A

Healing

Rosary

ANN FITCH

Illustrations by

Sr. Mary Grace Thul

Full Stop Press
Phoenix

Cover image © Ann Fitch
Cover and text design by: Amy Fitch
Interior art by: Sr. Mary Grace Thul

ISBN-10: 06-158-4344-1
ISBN-13: 978-0-61584-344-5

Printed in the United States of America

Published by:
Full Stop Press
P.O. Box 71784
Phoenix, AZ 85050
www.FullStopPress.com

Special Thanks

I would like to thank my family for tolerating the hours I spent working on this book. They are my joy and I appreciate all the time they sacrificed with me so that I could complete this book. I'd like to give special thanks to my daughter, Amy, for making such a fantastic cover for me.

With gratitude, I'd like to acknowledge an incredible artist, Sr. Mary Grace Thul. Her deeply touching artwork has been used throughout this book. She is a gifted Dominican sister who praises God through her art. Her art can be viewed and purchased in various formats on her web site:

http://www.sistermarygrace.artspan.com

The proceeds from her art help support her monastery. Sister Mary Grace Thul lives at the Caterina Benincasa Dominica Monastery in New Castle, Delaware.

Table of Contents

Introduction

Our Lord desires for each one of us to know Him intimately in His Triune form. He wants to bring us to the joy and peace of wholeness in Himself, His Holy Spirit and Our loving Father. Our Lord wishes to pour into our hearts true love for Him, trust in Our Father's will for us, and the wisdom and fire of His Holy Spirit so we can walk more confidently in faith with Him.

One simple way to begin allowing the Lord more fully into our hearts, minds, and spirits is to pray the Rosary. As we meditate on each mystery, we become more fully aware of how Our Lord lived His life and sought to please His Father in all that He did. What a marvelous example of faith and trust.

Through the Rosary Our Lord becomes more real to us, more human. As we meditate on both His humanity and divinity we grow in our understanding of how He wishes to lead us through His Holy Spirit to a deep and childlike relationship with His Father, Our Father. He said, ***"Unless you turn and become like children, you will not enter the kingdom of heaven."*** (Matthew 18:3) So like small children, let us take Our Father's hand and allow Him to touch every area of our lives with His all-encompassing love.

The Rosary also gives us a wonderful example of trust and faith in Our Lady. It is inspiring and helpful to meditate on how she allowed Our Lord to fully manifest Himself in her life. She humbly embraced all that God asked of her and through her example we can learn how to trust and walk a more complete faith journey.

With the Rosary we have an intercessor with Our Mother in heaven, Mary. What a blessing to have her go before the throne of God and intercede on our behalf. The Rosary is not a prayer to Mary. It is a prayer to God with Mary interceding for us. Our Lady always directs us to the Holy Trinity and away from herself to unity with God. She is the Mediatrix of grace not the source of all grace. Pope Pius XII in a radio message in 1953 said, "Whenever we speak of Mary or speak to her, let us not forget that she is really our Mother, for through her we received divine life. She gave us Jesus himself, the source of grace. Mary is the Mediatrix and Dispenser of graces." All graces she pours forth upon us are first and foremost from God, given through her to us.

Our Lady takes our prayers and petitions and lays them at the feet of Our Lord. She intercedes on our behalf, asking Jesus through His loving mercy to grant our desires according to Our Father's will. She always listens, always loves, always prays for that which is best for us, that which is Our Father's will for us.

All our prayers are heard and all our prayers are answered, just not always as we wish for them to be answered. Often our prayers are answered in a way that differs from what we wanted. Clearly what we wanted was not what God desired for us in that moment. And sometimes we are given exactly what we prayed for. In those moments our desires were in unison with God's divine will for us.

We know that the Lord has told us to be vigilant and watch the state of our hearts, minds and souls because there, *"Are the sources of life."* (Proverbs 4:23) It is our interior state that dictates our attitude which then determines how we live our lives and our state of grace. Jesus said, *"A good person out of the store of goodness in his heart produces good, but an evil person out of a store of evil produces evil; for from the fullness of the heart the mouth speaks."* (Luke 6:45 NAB) The question is how much good and evil are stored in our hearts? We have all been broken, we have all been hurt, it's what we choose to do with our hurt and brokenness that matters.

It is in our hearts, minds and souls that the Holy Spirit takes up residence. It is there that we need to clean house, so that the fruits of the Spirit, *"Love, joy, peace, patience, kindness, generosity, faithfulness, gentleness, and self-control,"* (Galatians 5:22) are what are evident in our lives. We need to clear out all the bad that keeps us from loving ourselves, others and God, so that the Holy Spirit can bless, lead and guide us more fully each day. No matter what condition your heart, mind, and soul are in, God can and will touch and heal you if you simply ask. Jesus said, *"Very truly, I tell you, if you ask anything of the Father in my name, he will give it to you."* (John 15:23) Allow God into the deepest parts of your heart, mind and soul to bring you inner healing and new freedom, *"And let the peace of Christ rule in your hearts."* (Colossians 3:15) God said, *"I will give you a new heart, and a new spirit I will put within you."* (Ezekiel 36:26 NAB) Believe that God will move and you will be moved.

In this healing Rosary please take your time. Do not rush. Allow the Lord to touch you, heal you, and bring you into wholeness through the power of His Holy Spirit. After you read the reflection, stop to reflect. Pause and invite the Lord to illuminate the experiences He wishes to illuminate.

If a memory surfaces, stop and ask the Lord to walk through that memory with you with His Holy Spirit

3

illuminating every aspect of that memory. If more than one memory surfaces, stay with that mystery until you have allowed the Lord to bless, touch, transform and heal whichever memories you recall through the power of His Holy Spirit. Our Lord wishes you to allow yourself to be touched and healed of your pain; be that physical, emotional, mental or spiritual pain. In his lifetime He, *"Cured all the sick, to fulfill what had been said by Isaiah the prophet: He took away our infirmities and bore our diseases."* (Matthew 8:16-17)

With the Lord there is no time frame. He is timeless and ever-present, *"Jesus Christ is the same yesterday, today, and forever."* (Hebrews 13:8) Do not concern yourself with how much time it takes you to pray through a mystery of the Rosary or even with completing a whole series of mysteries. Rather, come away with the Lord by yourself to a quiet place and rest in His love for you. Our Father knows what you need before you even ask. So, *"Ask and it will be given to you; seek and you will find; knock and the door will be opened to you. For everyone who asks, receives; and the one who seeks, finds; and to the one who knocks, the door will be opened."* (Matthew 7:7-8)

Jesus said, *"Do not let your hearts be troubled or afraid."* (John 14:27) So have no fear as you walk through your memories with Our Lord. Let Him heal you through the power of His Holy Spirit. For once you are healed and you walk more intimately with God in His Triune form, He will be able to work more powerfully in you and through you blessing your life and those around you. May these Rosary meditations lead you to a deeper, more childlike relationship with God, Our loving Father, Jesus, Our Lord and the Holy Spirit. And, may they bring you the healing you need in every aspect of your life.

Prayer

Dear heavenly Father, pour Your love out into my heart. Transform me by the power of Your Holy Spirit into a more beautiful child of Yours. May I come to know Your Son, my Lord, in a new, more intimate way. Let Your Holy Spirit pour out every gift and grace upon me.

Dearest Jesus, please lead me to a more loving union with You. Present me to Our Father, and help me to open more fully to the wisdom and power of Your Holy Spirit. Give me the courage to work with You through the healing process. Bring me to wholeness in every aspect of my life.

Mother Mary, may you always lead me to the Most Holy Trinity. Help me to humble myself before God as you do and be there as a loving mother always interceding for me before the throne of God.

Through these meditations of the Rosary may I receive spiritual, psychological, emotional and physical healing. Thank You for the graces that will be poured out upon me. Thank You for the blessings I will be given. May I be an example of love wherever I go. Amen.

The Rosary

The Rosary is a beautiful form of prayer. Rosary means "crown of roses". It is meant to be a spiritual crown of roses woven from the very prayers we pray as we pray the Rosary. Once complete, we then present the crown of roses to Our Lady in our hearts.

The Rosary is composed of mental prayer and vocal prayer. Mental prayer is meditation upon the mysteries of Jesus' life, death, resurrection, and ascension and upon the life of His Mother, Mary, and vocal prayer is just that, prayer said out loud.

The Rosary was originally given to St. Dominic by Our Blessed Mother to help in the conversion of sinners and the defeat of heresy. It was propagated by Blessed Alan de la Roche of the Dominican Order and over time the meditations on the Joyful, Sorrowful, and Glorious Mysteries were formulated. The Luminous Mysteries were added by Blessed Pope John Paul II. They were introduced in his Apostolic Letter, *Rosarium Virginis Mariae*, in October 2002.

Traditionally, the Joyful Mysteries have been recited on Mondays and Thursdays, the Sorrowful Mysteries have been recited on Tuesday and Friday, and the Glorious Mysteries have been recited on Wednesdays, Saturdays and Sundays. Blessed Pope John Paul II suggested that the Luminous Mysteries be said on Thursdays. Of course, all the mysteries of the Rosary could be said daily if one desires to do so.

If Praying without the Luminous Mysteries:

Monday – Joyful Mysteries
Tuesday – Sorrowful Mysteries
Wednesday – Glorious Mysteries
Thursday – Joyful Mysteries
Friday – Sorrowful Mysteries
Saturday – Glorious Mysteries
Sunday – Glorious Mysteries

If Praying with the Luminous Mysteries:

Monday – Joyful Mysteries
Tuesday – Sorrowful Mysteries
Wednesday – Glorious Mysteries
Thursday – Luminous Mysteries
Friday – Sorrowful Mysteries
Saturday – Glorious Mysteries
Sunday – Glorious Mysteries

If Praying all 20 Mysteries in one day:

Joyful Mysteries
Luminous Mysteries
Sorrowful Mysteries
Glorious Mysteries

Prayers of the Rosary

The Rosary is begun with the Sign of the Cross, which is the sign of Jesus' victory over sin and death. Following, is the Apostle's Creed (Symbolum Apostolorum), which is the foundation of Catholic belief. In addition, there are four other prayers: the Our Father (Pater Noster or Lord's Prayer), the Hail Mary (Ave Maria), the Glory Be (Gloria), and the Hail Holy Queen (Salve Regina).

The Our Father was given to us by Jesus Himself as an example of how we are to pray. The Hail Mary is composed of the words the angel Gabriel spoke to Mary at the Annunciation, the words St. Elizabeth spoke to Mary when she was filled with the Holy Spirit at the Visitation, and the words given to us by the Council of Ephesus (which declared Mary as the Mother of God or Theotokos). These two prayers along with the Glory Be are the most repeated prayers during the recitation of the Rosary. It is concluded with the Hail Holy Queen, O God, and the Pardon Prayer.

There are two optional prayers that were given to the children at Fatima that can be included in the recitation of the Rosary. The first is the Decade Prayer, which is said after the recitation of the prayers for each decade of the Rosary. The second is the Pardon Prayer said at the conclusion of the Rosary.

Sign of the Cross

In the name of the Father, and of the Son, and of the Holy Spirit. Amen.

Apostles' Creed

I believe in God the Father almighty, Creator of heaven and earth, and in Jesus Christ, his only Son, our Lord, who was conceived by the Holy Spirit, born of the Virgin Mary, suffered under Pontius Pilate, was crucified, died and was buried; He descended into hell; on the third day he rose again from the dead; he ascended into heaven, and is seated at the right hand of God the Father almighty; from there he will come to judge the living and the dead. I believe in the Holy Spirit, the holy Catholic Church, the communion of saints, the forgiveness of sins, the resurrection of the body, and life everlasting. Amen.

Our Father

Our Father, Who art in heaven, hallowed be Thy name; Thy kingdom come; Thy will be done on earth as it is in heaven. Give us this day our daily bread; and forgive us our trespasses as we forgive those who trespass against us; and lead us not into temptation, but deliver us from evil. Amen.

Hail Mary

Hail Mary, full of grace. The Lord is with thee. Blessed art thou among women, and blessed is the fruit of thy womb, Jesus. Holy Mary, Mother of God, pray for us sinners, now and at the hour of our death. Amen.

Glory Be

Glory be to the Father, and to the Son, and to the Holy Spirit, as it was in the beginning, is now, and ever shall be, world without end. Amen.

Decade Prayer

O my Jesus, forgive us our sins; save us from the fires of hell; lead all souls into Heaven, especially those who are in most need of thy mercy.

Hail Holy Queen

Hail, Holy Queen, Mother of mercy, our life, our sweetness and our hope. To thee do we cry, poor banished children of Eve: to thee do we send up our sighs, mourning and weeping in this valley of tears. Turn then, most gracious Advocate, thine eyes of mercy toward us, and after this our exile, show unto us the blessed fruit of thy womb, Jesus. O clement, O loving, O sweet Virgin Mary! Pray for us, O Holy Mother of God, that we may be made worthy of the promises of Christ. Amen.

O God

O God, whose only begotten Son, by His life, death, and resurrection, has purchased for us the rewards of eternal life, grant, we beseech Thee, that meditating upon these mysteries of the Most Holy Rosary of the Blessed Virgin Mary, we may imitate what they contain and obtain what they promise, through the same Christ Our Lord. Amen.

Pardon Prayer

My God, I believe, I adore, I trust, and I love Thee! I beg pardon for those who do not believe, do not adore, do not trust, and do not love Thee.

15 Promises

These 15 promises are said to have been given to St. Dominic and Blessed Alan de la Roche by Our Lady for those who pray the Rosary. They are comforting, filled with maternal love and protection, and provide us with another glimpse at the mercy of God.

1. *Whoever shall faithfully serve me by the recitation of the Rosary, shall receive signal graces.*

2. *I promise my special protection and the greatest graces to all who shall recite the Rosary.*

3. *The Rosary shall be a powerful armor against hell, it will destroy vice, decrease sin, and defeat heresies.*

4. *It will cause virtue and good works to flourish; it will obtain for souls the abundant mercy of God; it will withdraw the hearts of men from the love of the world and its vanities, and will lift them to the desire of eternal things. Oh, that souls would sanctify themselves by this means.*

5. *The soul which recommends itself to me by the recitation of the Rosary, shall not perish.*

6. *Whoever shall recite the Rosary devoutly, applying himself to the consideration of its sacred mysteries, shall never be conquered by misfortune. God will not chastise him in His justice, he shall not perish by an unprovided death; if he be just he shall remain in the grace of God, and become worthy of eternal life.*

7. *Whoever shall have a true devotion for the Rosary shall not die without the Sacraments of the Church.*

8. *Those who are faithful in reciting the Rosary shall have during their life and at their death the light of God and the plentitude of His graces; at the moment of death they shall participate in the merits of the saints in paradise.*

9. *I shall deliver from purgatory, those who have been devoted to the Rosary.*

10. *The faithful children of the Rosary shall merit a high degree of glory in Heaven.*

11. *You shall obtain all you ask of me by the recitation of the Rosary.*

12. *All those who propagate the holy Rosary shall be aided by Me in their necessities.*

13. *I have obtained from my Divine Son, that all the advocates of the Rosary shall have for intercessors, the entire celestial court during their life and at the hour of death.*

14. *All who recite the Rosary are my sons, and brothers of my only son Jesus Christ.*

15. *Devotion to my Rosary is a great sign of predestination.*

Feast Days of the Rosary

The Rosary is a meditation on all of the major events in the lives of Jesus and Mary. Each Mystery has a feast day associated with it, and each feast day is celebrated by the Church liturgically. Here is a chart of every Mystery and its associated liturgical feast.

Joyful Mysteries

Rosary Mystery	Feast Name	Feast Date
The Annunciation	Feast of the Annunciation	March 25
The Visitation	Feast of the Visitation	May 31
The Nativity	Christmas	December 25
The Presentation	Feast of the Presentation	February 2
The Finding in the Temple	Feast of the Holy Family	December 30

Luminous Mysteries

Rosary Mystery	Feast Name	Feast Date
The Baptism in the Jordan	Feast of the Baptism of the Lord	Sunday after the Epiphany
The Wedding at Cana	Feast of the Wedding at Cana	2nd Sunday after the Epiphany
The Proclamation of the Kingdom	Feast of Christ the King	Last Sunday in Ordinary Time
The Transfiguration	Feast of the Transfiguration	August 6
The Institution of the Eucharist	Feast of Corpus Christi	2nd Sunday after Pentecost

Sorrowful Mysteries

Rosary Mystery	Feast Name	Feast Date
The Agony in the Garden	Holy Thursday	Varies
The Scourging	Good Friday	Varies
The Crowning with Thorns	Feast of the Crowning with Thorns	Friday after Ash Wednesday
The Carrying of the Cross	Triumph of the Cross	September 14
The Crucifixion	Good Friday	Varies

Glorious Mysteries

Rosary Mystery	Feast Name	Feast Date
The Resurrection	Easter	Varies
The Ascension	Ascension Thursday	40 Days after Easter
The Descent of the Holy Spirit	Pentecost	50 Days after Easter
The Assumption	Feast of the Assumption	August 15
The Coronation	Feast of the Coronation	August 22

Saint Quotes About the Rosary

Throughout history many saints have had special love and devotion to Our Blessed Mother. They faithfully prayed the Rosary on a daily basis. Here are a few quotes from them.

1. *"The Rosary is a priceless treasure inspired by God."*
   St. Louis De Montfort

2. *"The holy Rosary is a powerful weapon. Use it with confidence and you'll be amazed at the results."*
   St. Josemaria Escriva

3. *"If you say the Holy Rosary every day, with a spirit of faith and love, our Lady will make sure she leads you very far along her Son's path."* St. Josemaria Escriva

4. *"The Rosary is the 'weapon' for these times."*
   St. Pio of Pietrelcina

5. *"Some people are so foolish that they think they can go through life without the help of the Blessed Mother. Love the Madonna and pray the rosary, for her Rosary is the weapon against the evils of the world today. All graces given by God pass through the Blessed Mother."*
   St. Pio of Pietrelcina

6. *"Love the Madonna and pray the rosary, for her rosary is the weapon against the evils of the world today."*
   St. Pio of Pietrelcina

7. *"Our Lady has never refused me a grace through the recitation of the rosary."* St. Pio of Pietrelcina

8. *"Love the Blessed Mother and make her loved. Always recite the rosary."* St. Pio of Pietrelcina

9. *"The Holy Rosary is the storehouse of countless blessings."* Blessed Alan de la Roche

10. *"The greatest method of praying is to pray the Rosary."* St. Francis de Sales

11. *"When the Holy Rosary is said well, it gives Jesus and Mary more glory and is more meritorious than any other prayer."* St. Louis de Montfort

12. *"Recite your Rosary with faith, with humility, with confidence, and with perseverance."* St. Louis de Montfort

Popes Quotes About the Rosary

The Rosary is one of the most written about devotions by the popes. Many popes have recited the Rosary daily. Here are some quotes from them.

1. *"The Rosary is the most beautiful and richest of all prayers to the Mediatrix of all grace; it is the prayer that touches most the heart of the Mother of God. Say it each day."* Pope St. Pius X

2. *"Give me an army saying the Rosary and I will conquer the world."* Blessed Pope Pius IX

3. *"The rosary is the scourge of the devil."* Pope Adrian VI

4. *"The Rosary is a school for learning true Christian perfection."* Blessed Pope John XXIII

5. *"The rosary is a treasure of graces."* Pope Paul V

6. *"By its nature the recitation of the rosary calls for a quiet rhythm and a lingering peace, helping the individual to meditate on the mysteries of the Lord's life as grasped by the heart of her who was closer to the Lord than all others."* Blessed Pope John Paul II

7. *"The Rosary is the most excellent form of prayer and the most efficacious means of attaining eternal life. It is the remedy for all our evils, the root of all our blessings. There is no more excellent way of praying."* Pope Leo XIII

8. *"Among all the devotions approved by the Church none has been so favored by so many miracles as*

the devotion of the Most Holy Rosary." Blessed Pope Pius IX

9. *"The Rosary is my favorite prayer. A marvelous prayer! Marvelous in its simplicity and in its depth."* Blessed Pope John Paul II

10. *"The ultimate purpose of devotion to the Blessed Virgin is to glorify God and to lead Christians to commit themselves to a life which is in absolute conformity with His will."* Pope Paul VI

11. *"The Rosary offers an easy way to present the chief mysteries of the Christian religion and to impress them upon the mind."* Pope Leo XIII

12. *"The Rosary of the Blessed Virgin Mary, combining in a convenient and practical form an unexcelled form of prayer, an instrument well adapted to preserve the faith and an illustrious example of perfect virtue, should be often in the hands of the true Christian and be devoutly recited and meditated upon."* Pope Pious XI

13. *"We are convinced that the Rosary, if devoutly used, is bound to benefit not only the individual but society at large."* Pope Leo XIII

14. *"This prayer is well-suited to the devotion of the People of God, most pleasing to the Mother of God and most effective in gaining heaven's blessings."* Pope Paul VI

15. *"May the beads of the Rosary be in the hands of all."* Pope Pious XII

16. *"To recite the Rosary is nothing other than to contemplate with Mary the face of Christ."* Blessed Pope John Paul II

17. *"The Rosary belongs among the finest and most praiseworthy traditions of Christian contemplation."* Blessed Pope John Paul II

18. *"The Rosary helps us to be conformed ever more closely to Christ until we attain true holiness."* Blessed Pope John Paul II

19. *"When reciting the Rosary, the important and meaningful moments of salvation history are relived."* Pope Benedict XVI

20. *"The Rosary, when it is prayed in an authentic way, not mechanical and superficial but profoundly, it brings, in fact, peace and reconciliation. It contains within itself the healing power of the Most Holy Name of Jesus, invoked with faith and love at the centre of each 'Hail Mary'."* Pope Benedict XVI

How to Pray this Rosary

There are so many ways to pray the Rosary, but the mechanics remain consistent. The order of the recitation of prayers is not changed only the length of time for reflection and meditation. In this Rosary time is taken to pray through visualizations for inner healing before recitation of the Hail Marys. As mentioned previously, take your time and allow God to touch, bless, and heal you as you pray.

If you are new to reciting the Rosary these instructions should be very helpful. They will take you through praying one full set of mysteries. Do not allow yourself to become frustrated as you learn the mechanics, be patient with yourself as you learn this beautiful method of prayer.

1. While holding the crucifix, make the **Sign of the Cross** and then recite the **Apostles' Creed**.
2. Recite the **Our Father** on the first single bead.
3. Recite a **Hail Mary** on the next three beads for an increase in faith, hope, and love.
4. On the next single bead read the first Rosary mystery, read the accompanying scripture, and recite the **Our Father**.
5. Read the reflection and do the visualization.
6. Recite a **Hail Mary** on each of the next 10 beads while reflecting on the mystery. Complete this decade with the **Glory Be** and the **Decade Prayer**.

7. On the next single bead read the second Rosary mystery, read the accompanying scripture, and recite the **Our Father**.

8. Read the reflection and do the visualization.

9. Recite a **Hail Mary** on each of the next 10 beads while reflecting on the mystery. Complete this decade with the **Glory Be** and the **Decade Prayer**.

10. On the next single bead read the third Rosary mystery, read the accompanying scripture, and recite the **Our Father**.

11. Read the reflection and do the visualization.

12. Recite a **Hail Mary** on each of the next 10 beads while reflecting on the mystery. Complete this decade with the **Glory Be** and the **Decade Prayer**.

13. On the next single bead read the fourth Rosary mystery, read the accompanying scripture, and recite the **Our Father**.

14. Read the reflection and do the visualization.

15. Recite a **Hail Mary** on each of the next 10 beads while reflecting on the mystery. Complete this decade with the **Glory Be** and the **Decade Prayer**.

16. On the next single bead read the fifth Rosary mystery, read the accompanying scripture, and recite the **Our Father**.

17. Read the reflection and do the visualization.

18. Recite a **Hail Mary** on each of the next 10 beads while reflecting on the mystery. Complete this decade with the **Glory Be** and the **Decade Prayer**.

19. When the fifth mystery is complete, conclude by reciting the **Hail Holy Queen**, **O God**, and the **Pardon Prayer**.

The Joyful Mysteries

As you pray the Joyful Mysteries, open yourself to the healing power of the Holy Trinity. It is joy that God desires for you. Jesus said, *"If you keep my commandments, you will abide in my love, just as I have kept my Father's commandments and abide in his love. I have told these things to you so that my joy may be in you, and that your joy may be complete."* (John 15:10-11) The joy God has in store for you is beyond your wildest imaginings. It is a joy rooted in love and peace that surpasses all understanding.

Through these Joyful Mysteries seek to become a whole, peace-filled, joyful child of God. Trust in God's goodness and believe in His healing love. In His lifetime so many came to Him, trying to touch Him *"For power came out from him and healed all of them."* (Luke 6:19) Believe that Jesus can and will heal you because he said, *"For mortals it is impossible, but for God all things are possible."* (Matthew 19:26)

Prayer

Dearest Father, I now place myself in Your loving hands. Mold me into the child of light and love You created me to be. Replace all darkness in my life with the healing light of Your Son, and my Savior, Jesus Christ. Pour forth Your Holy Spirit upon me that I might truly be transformed and fortified.

Dearest Mother Mary, I come before you, seeking your assistance. Place your loving arms around me and carry me to your Son so that He can heal me in those areas of my heart, mind, body, and soul that are

in need of His healing touch. Help me, dearest Mother, to become humble and charitable. Teach me true detachment from the world so that I can be pure in heart, mind, body, and soul. Above all, help me to be an obedient child of God, ever mindful of His commands. Thank you, dearest Mother for your love and intercession.

May the most Holy Trinity be ever praised, honored and glorified. Amen.

Pray:

- ❖ **Sign of the Cross**
- ❖ **Apostles' Creed**
- ❖ **Hail Mary** (for an increase in faith)
- ❖ **Hail Mary** (for an increase in hope)
- ❖ **Hail Mary** (for an increase in love)
- ❖ **Glory Be**

First Joyful Mystery

The Annunciation

In the sixth month, the angel Gabriel was sent from God to a town of Galilee called Nazareth, to a virgin betrothed to a man named Joseph, of the house of David, and the virgin's name was Mary. And coming to her, he said, "Hail favored one! The Lord is with you." But she was greatly troubled at what was said and pondered what sort of greeting this might be. Then the angel said to her, "Do not be afraid, Mary, for you have found favor with God. Behold, you will conceive in your womb and bear a son, and you shall name him Jesus. He will be great and will be called the Son of the Most High, and the Lord God will give him the throne of his father David, and he will rule over the house of Jacob forever, and of his kingdom there will be no end." But Mary said to the angel, "How can this be, since I have no relations with a man?" And the angel said to her in reply, "The holy Spirit will come upon you, and the power of the Most High will overshadow you. Therefore the child to be born will be called holy, the Son of God. And behold, Elizabeth, your relative, has also conceived a son in her old age, and this is the sixth month for her who was called barren; for nothing will be impossible for God." Mary said, "Behold, I am the handmaid of the Lord. May it be done to me according to your word." Then the angel departed from her. (Luke 1:26-38 NAB)

Pray:

❖ Our Father

Traditionally associated with this mystery is the virtue of humility.

Humility is a misunderstood virtue. It is not being weak but being courageous and strong. It is a willingness to be honest before God and man no matter what the repercussions or ramifications might be. It is trusting in God's divine will and acceptance of that will. Humility leads the soul to recognize the presence of God within. It directs the soul to the realization that in its weakness and nothingness God is strong and powerful supplying every gift and grace needed to live a life full of love and peace. As St. Paul wrote, *"I can do all things through him who strengthens me."* (Philippians 4:13) We too will have all our needs met and surpassed if we are humble before the Lord.

One of the greatest acts of humility was Jesus choosing to allow Himself to become man and be born of Mary. Through that humble act He became human so He could teach us how to live, bring us salvation by dying on the cross for our sins, and through His resurrection bring us to everlasting life with Him. *"Let the same mind be in you that was in Christ Jesus, who, though he was in the form of God, did not regard equality with God as something to be exploited, but he emptied himself, taking the form of a slave, being born in human likeness. And being found in human form, he humbled himself and became obedient to the point of death – even death on a cross."* (Philippians 2:5-8)

Reflection:

Have you been told by your mother, father, or other family member that you were a surprise, an accident, a mistake or that you were not wanted? Were you placed in an adoptive home?

When you discovered that you were pregnant, how did you respond? Were you frightened, concerned that you were not ready to become a parent, that you were not emotionally, psychologically or financially ready to be responsible for another human being? Were you troubled that you would not be able to provide a sound environment for your child? Was the baby conceived outside of marriage or as a result of sexual assault? Did you question how this could be happening to you or wonder why me? Did you hope for a miscarriage? Did you lose the baby through miscarriage or abortion?

Perhaps your experience is just the opposite. Have you been told that you cannot have a child? Were your dreams of carrying a child in your womb shattered? Did you become angry with God, others, or yourself? Did you blame yourself or someone else? Did you think that God was punishing you for something you did in your life?

Visualizations:

For all:

Picture the Lord sitting with your mother who is pregnant with you. His hands are extended and He lovingly says, *"Before I formed you in the womb I knew you, and before you were born I consecrated you."* (Jeremiah 1:5) Feel His love flowing over you in your mother's womb filling it with light as He says, *"I have loved you with an everlasting love."* (Jeremiah 31:3) Feel your mother's love for you. Realize that you are a child of light and love, beautiful just as you are. Allow the Lord's love to wash away any hurt, anger or fear that you have carried and, *"Give yourself the esteem you deserve."* (Sirach 10:27)

Humbly forgive those who have wounded your image of yourself from conception and release them from any anger you may have felt towards them. For *"If you forgive the sins of any, they are forgiven them; if you retain the sins of any, they are retained."* (John 20:23) Accept God's love for you and know that you are perfectly formed in His image and likeness, that you are not a mistake, but a wanted, loved child of His. Jesus says to you, *"Do not fear, for I have redeemed you; I have called you by name: you are mine."* (Isaiah 43:1) Believe that you are His and trust that He will always love you.

For full-term pregnancies:

Think back to the moment(s) when you conceived. Picture your womb being filled with light and love. You feel an immense need to protect the life within you. A love unlike any other fills your heart and surrounds the baby within you. Jesus is standing before you with His arms extended and He says, *"Blessed are you among women, and blessed is the fruit of your womb."* (Luke 1:42) He gently touches you and you can feel His love blessing you and the child within you, healing you both of any negativity that may have affected you.

You say to the Lord, "Thank you for Your love and blessings, walk through this entire pregnancy with me and heal us of all hurt and negativity that may have affected us." Jesus smiles at you and nods saying, *"I am with you always."* (Matthew 28:20). You can feel His presence with you both every day, permeating every part of you, blessing and healing you both. You thank Him and say, *"I will praise the Lord as long as I live; I will sing praises to my God all my life long."* (Psalm 146:2)

For those who cannot conceive:

Picture yourself in the extra bedroom in your home, the room that would be a nursery. Jesus enters the room and with tears in your eyes you say to Him, *"O God, do not be far from me; O my God, make haste to help me."* (Psalm 71:12) You share with the Lord your hurt, your feelings of loss, your shattered dreams, your broken heart knowing that, *"He heals the brokenhearted, and binds up their wounds."* (Psalm 147:3)

The Lord reaches out and touches your head saying, *"My thoughts are not your thoughts, nor are your ways my ways."* (Isaiah 55:8) You can feel His light enveloping you bringing the understanding that you are not being punished, but that if you are called to it, you have a different road to take to parenthood, a road that brings light, love and life to all involved. Jesus pours forth His mercy upon you, filling you to overflowing. He says, *"May mercy, peace, and love be yours in abundance."* (Jude 1:2)

You know without a doubt that you are a loved, cherished child of God. You realize that if it's God's will for you He will open the way for you to become a parent but in His time and in His way. May, *"The Lord grant what is in your heart, fulfill your every plan."* (Psalm 20:5 NAB)

For those adopted:

Picture yourself sitting outdoors with Jesus. He is listening to you tell Him about your life as an adopted child. You turn to Him and ask Him to touch your heart and heal any sense of abandonment, anger, confusion, loss or rejection you have because you were placed in an adoptive home. He says, *"I am with you always."* (Matthew 28:20) *"I will never leave you or forsake*

33

you." (Hebrews 13:5) He reaches out and takes your hand in His. You can feel His love touching your heart, blessing you. He says to you, *"If you forgive others their trespasses, your heavenly Father will also forgive you."* (Matthew 6:14)

Even though it is hard, you forgive your birth parents for placing you in an adoptive home and not raising you themselves. As you forgive them you feel an enormous weight lifting off your shoulders and peace permeating your being. You realize how blessed you have been to be loved and cared for by your adoptive family and you ask the Lord to bless both your birth and adoptive parents.

Jesus looks at you and says, *"May mercy, peace, and love be yours in abundance."* (Jude 1:2) Light surrounds you and you feel an overwhelming sense of self-acceptance and love. You tell the Lord, *"I have indeed received much joy and encouragement from your love."* (Philemon 1:7) He smiles at you, blesses you and leaves.

For a miscarriage or abortion:

Imagine yourself in a nursery with Mary standing before you her arms extended to embrace you. Walk into her arms as she says, *"'My loyal child in faith: grace, mercy and peace from God the Father and Christ Jesus our Lord,'* (1 Timothy 1:2) *be with you."*

Picture Jesus walking through the nursery door holding an infant in His arms. As He draws near He hands you the child He has carried and you take your baby in your arms. You unwrap the baby and count his or her fingers and toes. You can smell that fresh baby scent as you caress your baby's face. As you bond with your baby, Mary wraps her loving arms around you both.

Feel her love pouring through you and feel the love you have for your child.

Jesus asks you, *"What name will you give this child?"* You name your baby. Jesus smiles and repeats the baby's name and says to him or her, ***"Before I formed you in the womb I knew you, and before you were born I consecrated you."*** (Jeremiah 1:5) Jesus looks at you and says, ***"I will restore you to health; of your wounds I will heal you."*** (Jeremiah 30:17) Feel His healing love fill you to overflowing. Embrace that love and accept it.

Kiss your baby's face and hug him or her tightly to your heart then hand your child back to the Lord. Ask Jesus to care for your child until you meet again. Know in your heart that your child is loved and cared for, protected and safe. ***"Now may the Lord of peace himself give you peace at all times in all ways."*** (2 Thessalonians 3:16)

Pray:

- ❖ **10 Hail Marys**
- ❖ **Glory Be**
- ❖ **Decade Prayer**

The Second Joyful Mystery
The Visitation

During those days Mary set out and traveled to the hill country in haste to a town of Judah, where she entered the house of Zechariah and greeted Elizabeth. When Elizabeth heard Mary's greeting, the infant leaped in her womb, and Elizabeth, filled with the holy Spirit, cried out in a loud voice and said, "Most blessed are you among women, and blessed is the fruit of your womb. And how does this happen to me, that the mother of my Lord should come to me? For at the moment the sound of your greeting reached my ears, the infant in my womb leaped for joy. Blessed are you who believed that what was spoken to you by the Lord would be fulfilled." (Luke 1:39-45 NAB)

Mary remained with her about three months and then returned to her home. (Luke 1:56 NAB)

Pray:

❖ **Our Father**

Traditionally associated with this mystery is the virtue of charity.

Charity has two parts, love of God and love of man. It begins with allowing ourselves to be loved by God Our Father as His children and by Jesus as His brothers and sisters. It then manifests itself in outward displays of love for others just as God has loved us. When we act in charity towards another there is no desire for reciprocity or reward. The act is done as if it is being done by God,

37

through us, towards Himself in others. We are transparent and God's love flows through us to Himself in others. As God gives selflessly to us we choose by charity to selflessly give to others. At times this will require sacrifice. But isn't this exactly the kind of love we are called to in Christ, a sacrificial love that removes all reward for us and implies that we desire what is best for another above ourselves?

Charity is not always giving to others. It is also allowing others the joy of giving to us, humbly accepting what others wish to do for us. It is also loving ourselves as God loves us, completely.

Reflection:

When a family member, friend or even a stranger approached you asking for help, did you help? Did you feel taken advantage of, or were you upset by their asking? Did you question whether they really needed your help or judge them?

When you sought help from a relative or friend did you receive the love, financial support, food or shelter you needed? Were you turned away? When denied help, did you feel rejected, humiliated, unimportant, or without value?

When others have seen a need and have desired to give to you, have you humbly accepted their help or rejected it?

<u>Visualization:</u>

Picture the Lord standing in front of you, saying, *"You are precious in my sight, and honored, and I love you."* (Isaiah 43:4) Look into His eyes, filled with love and compassion, and feel the love He has for you.

Now picture with you those people to whom you did not show true charity. As you look at each person, he or she changes into an image of Jesus. You realize that by helping them you would have shown charity towards Jesus. Look each one in the eyes and ask their forgiveness. As each one extends forgiveness to you embrace that forgiveness and feel it's healing warmth. Feel God's love enveloping you, blessing you.

In this moment picture in your mind anyone from whom you sought help emotionally, financially, and/or physically who refused to help you. Look into their eyes, and without judging them, tell them how they hurt you, upset you or made you feel worthless when you most needed their help. Hear them say, "I'm sorry." Accept their apology and tell them you forgive them.

See God's light filling the area you are standing in. Allow that light to fill your heart, mind, body and soul. Thank the Lord for giving you the grace to forgive and let go. Thank Him for presenting you with opportunities to love others as you love Him. Thank Him for the times when others have loved and helped you. Open your heart and receive with joy all that God desires to give you at this very moment. Feel His love permeate your soul, His peace fill you to overflowing. *__Give thanks to the Lord, for he is good, for his steadfast love endures forever.__* (Psalm 106:1)

Pray:

- ❖ **10 Hail Marys**
- ❖ **Glory Be**
- ❖ **Decade Prayer**

The Third Joyful Mystery

The Nativity

In those days a decree went out from Caesar Augustus that the whole world should be enrolled. This was the first enrollment, when Quirinius was governor of Syria. So all went to be enrolled, each to his own town. And Joseph too went up from Galilee from the town of Nazareth to Judea, to the city of David that is called Bethlehem, because he was of the house and family of David to be enrolled with Mary, his betrothed, who was with child. While they were there, the time came for her to have her child, and she gave birth to her firstborn son. She wrapped him in swaddling clothes and laid him in a manger, because there was no room for them in the inn.

Now there were shepherds in that region living in the fields and keeping the night watch over their flock. The angel of the Lord appeared to them and the glory of the Lord shone around them, and they were struck with great fear. The angel said to them, "Do not be afraid; for behold, I proclaim to you good news of great joy that will be for all the people. For today in the city of David a savior has been born for you who is Messiah and Lord. And this will be a sign for you: you will find an infant wrapped in swaddling clothes and lying in a manger." And suddenly there was a multitude of the heavenly host with the angel, praising God and saying:

> *Glory to God in the highest*
> *and on earth peace to those on whom*
> *his favor rests.*

When the angels went away from them to heaven, the shepherds said to one another, "Let us go, then, to Bethlehem to see this thing that has taken place, which the Lord has made known to us." So they went in haste and found Mary and Joseph, and the infant lying in the manger. When they saw this, they made known the message that had been told them about this child. All who heard it were amazed by what had been told them by the shepherds. And Mary kept all these things, reflecting on them in her heart. Then the shepherds returned, glorifying and praising God for all they had heard and seen, just as it had been told to them. (Luke 2:1-20 NAB)

Pray:

❖ **Our Father**

Traditionally associated with this mystery is the virtue of detachment from the world.

Jesus said, *"Do not worry about your life, what you will eat or what you will drink, or about your body, what you will wear. Is not life more than food and the body more than clothing? But strive first for the kingdom of God and his righteousness, and all these things will be given to you as well."* (Matthew 6:25,33) Jesus did not want us worrying about things of this earth. Rather, He wanted us to seek union with God above all else. He promised that if we sought Him and His righteousness all our needs would be supplied.

Our life here is temporary, but life after death is eternal. St. John wrote, *"And the world and its desires are passing away, but those who do the will of God live forever."* (1 John 2:17) Our task while on earth is not to allow ourselves to become unduly attached to others, things, or ways of thinking. Instead, we are to put our trust in God's love and be obedient to His will for us. May we, together with the psalmist say, *"Teach me to do your will, for you are my God. Let your good spirit lead me on a level path."* (Psalm 143:10)

Reflection:

What are you attached to: your job; money; your earthly possessions; your relatives or friends; alcohol or drugs; your way of thinking; resentment, anger, bitterness; sexual desires or fantasies? What is it that you cannot let go of? What is keeping you from an intimate relationship with God?

Visualization:

Picture yourself standing before the Lord, as He lies sleeping in the manger. Think of the things, people, or ways of thinking that you are most attached to. Of those, what would you like to give to Jesus?

Step toward Him. Fall to your knees in adoration.

Ask Jesus for the courage and strength you need to give Him all that you are, all that you have, and all that has kept you from Him. For, *"Deliverance belongs to the Lord."* (Jonah 2:10) Cry out to Him, *"Heal me O Lord, and I shall be healed; save me, and I shall be saved, for you are my praise."* (Jeremiah 17:14) As you look at Him, He is smiling at you. His tiny hands are reaching out to you with love, mercy and forgiveness. Feel the power of His love melt your heart. Experience His peace as it comes over you, filling you.

Thank Jesus for giving you the courage and strength you need to place Him before all earthly possessions, relationships, and ways of thinking. Accept the grace He is pouring out upon you to seek Him first. Give, *"Glory to God in the highest,"* (Luke 2:14) and, *"Thanks to God unceasingly."* (1 Thessalonians 2:13 NAB)

Pray:

- ❖ **10 Hail Marys**
- ❖ **Glory Be**
- ❖ **Decade Prayer**

The Fourth Joyful Mystery
The Presentation

When the days were completed for their purification according to the law of Moses, they took him up to Jerusalem to present him to the Lord, just as it is written in the law of the Lord, "Every male that opens the womb shall be consecrated to the Lord," and to offer the sacrifice of "a pair of turtledoves or two young pigeons," in accordance with the dictate in the law of the Lord.

Now there was a man in Jerusalem whose name was Simeon. This man was righteous and devout, awaiting the consolation of Israel, and the holy Spirit was upon him. It had been revealed to him by the holy Spirit that he should not see death before he had seen the Messiah of the Lord. He came in the Spirit into the temple; and when the parents brought in the child Jesus to perform the custom of the law in regard to him, he took him into his arms and blessed God, saying: "Now, Master, you may let your servant go in peace, according to your word, for my eyes have seen your salvation, which you prepared in sight of all the peoples, a light for revelation to the Gentiles, and glory for your people Israel."

The child's father and mother were amazed at what was said about him; and Simeon blessed them and said to Mary his mother, "Behold, this child is destined for the fall and rise of many in Israel, and to be a sign that will be contradicted (and you yourself a sword will pierce) so that the thoughts of many hearts may be revealed." There was also a prophetess, Anna, the daughter of Phanuel, of the tribe of Asher. She was advanced in years, having lived seven years with her husband after her marriage, and then as a widow until she was eighty-four. She never left the temple, but worshiped night and day with fasting and prayer. And coming forward at that very time, she gave thanks to God and spoke about the child to all who were awaiting the redemption of Jerusalem. (Luke 2:22-38 NAB)

Pray:

❖ **Our Father**

Traditionally associated with this mystery is the virtue of purity of heart: charity, chastity, love of truth, and orthodoxy of faith.

God wants all of His children to love Him and obey His commandments, especially the commandments of love, and to have true charity towards themselves and others. Jesus said, *"They who have my commandments and keep them are those who love me; and those who love me will be loved by my Father, and I will love them and reveal myself to them."* (John 14:21)

In the book of Proverbs it is written, *"Above all else, guard your heart, for everything you do flows from it."* (Proverbs 4:23 NAB) It is through acquiring purity of heart that God infuses His light within us and opens us to receive wisdom and truth so we can see Him in our lives and in our deaths. For Jesus said, *"Blessed are the pure in heart, for they will see God."* (Matthew 5:8)

Through the sacrament of Baptism we are washed clean in body, mind, heart and soul and filled with sanctifying grace. We are brought into the family of God and are filled with the Holy Spirit Who leads us to truth and fills us with faith. We are asked through the sacrament of Confirmation to become responsible for our relationship with God, to allow the gifts of the Holy Spirit to become manifest in our lives, and to live our Baptismal promises. Since we are God's children through Baptism, we know that if we are tempted to turn away from our faith, live immodestly or act or think impurely, *"God is faithful, and he will not let you be tested beyond your strength, but with the testing he will also provide the way out so that you may be able to endure it."* (1 Corinthians 10:13)

We are called to be chaste and modest in our speech, in our actions, in our thoughts, and in our use of social medias. In this world there are innumerable temptations against chastity: unclean jokes and language; web sites and games, television programs, movies, books, and musical lyrics that suggest and promote immodest dress, sexual promiscuity, lustful desires, premarital sex and adultery. St. Paul wrote, *"Do you not know that your body is a temple of the holy Spirit within you, which you have from God, and that you are not your own? For you were bought with a price; therefore glorify God in your body."* (1 Corinthians 6:19-20) Chastity and modesty are challenged on every front so, *"Keep awake and pray that you may not come into the time of trial; the spirit indeed is willing, but the flesh is weak."* (Mark 14:38) Remember, *"The body, however, is not for immorality, but for the Lord."* (1 Corinthians 6:13 NAB) for, *"God did not call us to impurity but to holiness."* (1 Thessalonians 4:7)

Reflection:

We are called, as children of God, not to conform to the ways of the world. Instead, we are called to be holy in body, mind, heart, and soul. *"Let the same mind be in you that was in Christ Jesus."* (Philippians 2:5) To help yourself choose to be holy ask yourself before you act, "By doing this would I be giving honor and glory to God? Would I be acting in a way that is faithful to the Church's teachings?" If the answer is no, then rethink what you are about to do and ask God to give you the grace to change what you have planned to do to something that does honor and glorify Him and does follow the Church's teachings.

Sexual purity and chastity are virtues of love, true self-sacrificing love of self and others. Countless temptations exist and faithfulness to sexual purity is difficult but not impossible. Keeping faithful to our desire for purity can sometimes become skewed or lost completely by our thoughts and/or actions.

Do you dress modestly or avoid inappropriate conversations? Do you tell lewd jokes? Do you listen to sexually charged songs? Do you have impure thoughts and willfully act on them? Do you visit pornographic websites or view pornographic materials? Do you play video games or watch TV shows and/or movies that emphasize sexual manipulation of others or promote impure behaviors? Do you engage in premarital or extramarital sex? Has someone else exposed you to or pressured you into acting impurely? Has someone taken your innocence and purity through molestation or rape? Do you feel defiled, guilty or unworthy of God's love?

Visualizations:

For All:

Picture yourself walking along a beautiful wooded path with Jesus. As you walk along He tells you there is nothing His Father, your Father will not forgive you, if you but ask. Trusting His words you begin to tell Him of all the impure things you have said and done in the past, any ways you have not been faithful to the Church's teachings. With compassion, Jesus takes your hand in His own, and with love He gives you the grace to say, *"Have mercy on me, O God, according to your steadfast love; according to your abundant mercy blot out my transgressions. Wash me thoroughly from my iniquity, and cleanse me from my sin. Do not cast me away from your presence, and do not take your holy spirit from me. Restore to me the joy of your salvation, and sustain in me a willing spirit."* (Psalm 51: 1-2,11-12) Feel Jesus' mercy falling upon you and His love and grace filling you to overflowing. Allow the Holy Spirit to descend upon you, filling you with peace and love, renewing you.

As you come to a clearing you see the Father standing before you. With His arms outstretched to embrace you He says, *"Come, share in your master's joy."* (Matthew 25:28 NAB) As you walk into His embrace He whispers, *"There will be more joy in heaven over one sinner who repents than over ninety-nine righteous persons who need no repentance."* (Luke 15:7) As He holds you away from Himself, smiling, He looks into your eyes and says, *"Here is my servant, whom I have chosen, my beloved, with whom my soul is well pleased."* (Matthew 12:18) Allow the Lord's forgiveness to flow over you in gentle waves. Forgive yourself just as God has forgiven you. *"Give thanks to the Lord, for he is good; his steadfast love endures forever."* (Psalm 118:1)

If you have been molested or raped:

Imagine yourself in your favorite place being held by the Blessed Mother. Jesus is standing nearby. Feel Mary's loving arms around you, her peace filling you.

Gently she carries you to her Son for healing.

If you can, allow Jesus to walk with you back to the time(s) you were molested or raped. Feel His gentle love surrounding you as He takes you in His loving arms. Allow the Lord's compassion to form a safe cocoon around you and provide a place where your perpetrator cannot touch you. As He does that He holds your hand gently in His own.

As you begin to experience the feelings you did when you were molested or raped let the Lord's healing love wipe away the feelings of fear, being dominated, controlled or overpowered. Hear the Lord gently say, *"For I, the Lord your God, hold your right hand; it is I who say to you, 'Do not fear, I will help you.'"* (Isaiah 41:13) Jesus is right there with you, loving you, accepting you, healing you. Give the Lord your feelings of helplessness, anger, confusion, sadness, anxiety, fear, distrust, guilt, humiliation, vulnerability, and/or shame. Let Him wipe away your tears as He says, *"Cease your cries of mourning, wipe the tears from your eyes"* (Jeremiah 31:16 NAB) *"For I am the Lord who heals you."* (Exodus 15:26)

Take your time. Jesus wants you to experience His healing presence for as long as you need it. See Him taking any negative feelings you have had away from you and replacing them with self-love, self-acceptance, freedom, self-control, confidence, security, strength, and peace.

Jesus softly whispers to you, *"pray for those who abuse you...Be merciful, just as your Father is merciful...do not condemn, and you will not be condemned. Forgive, and you will be forgiven."* (Luke 6:28,36,37) Quietly, as best you can, forgive the person who assaulted you and ask the Lord for the grace to no longer condemn or judge yourself or your assailant. Feel Jesus' loving mercy flowing over you, filling you from the top of your head to the tips of your toes. Embrace the graces being poured out upon you – hope, trust, joy, tranquility, courage, self-respect, clarity, innocence, purity, and love.

With great care, Jesus hands you back to our Blessed Mother. She gently wipes away your tears, soothing you, accepting you exactly as you are, blameless. After a few moments she looks you in the eyes and says, *"God is our refuge and our strength, an ever-present help in distress. For to his angels he has given command about you, that they guard you in all your ways."* (Psalm 46:2, Psalm 91:11 NAB) Then she kisses your forehead and slowly she and Jesus walk away from you, leaving you peaceful and calm.

Pray:

- ❖ **10 Hail Marys**
- ❖ **Glory Be**
- ❖ **Decade Prayer**

The Fifth Joyful Mystery
The Finding in the Temple

Each year his parents went to Jerusalem for the feast of Passover, and when he was twelve years old, they went up according to festival custom. After they had completed its days, as they were returning, the boy Jesus remained behind in Jerusalem, but his parents did not know it. Thinking that he was in the caravan, they journeyed for a day and looked for him among their relatives and acquaintances, but not finding him, they returned to Jerusalem to look for him. After three days they found him in the temple, sitting in the midst of the teachers, listening to them and asking them questions, and all who heard him were astounded at his understanding and his answers. When his parents saw him, they were astonished, and his mother said to him, "Son, why have you done this to us? Your father and I have been looking for you with great anxiety." And he said to them, "Why were you looking for me? Did you not know that I must be in my Father's house?" But they did not understand what he said to them. He went down with them and came to Nazareth, and was obedient to them; and his mother kept all these things in her heart. And Jesus advanced in wisdom and age and favor before God and man. (Luke 2:41-52 NAB)

Pray:

❖ Our Father

Traditionally associated with this mystery is the virtue of obedience to God's will.

Obedience to God's will is an inward and outward expression of our love for God, Who is love. Very simply, if we love Him, we will obey Him. Jesus said, *"If you love me, you will keep my commandments. And I will ask the Father, and he will give you another Advocate to be with you forever. This is the Spirit of truth."* (John 14:15-17)   Obedience is the true test of our love for Christ and the secret to discovering God's will for our lives in the wisdom of the Holy Spirit.

God is all-powerful and all knowing.   His will is perfect and always best. It is written, *"For surely I know the plans I have for you, says the Lord, plans for your welfare, not for harm, to give you a future with hope."* (Jeremiah 29:11) God in His love always wants what is best for us, that which will bring us closer to Him that which will bring peace and joy to our lives.

But what exactly are we to obey? Jesus makes that clear for us; *"You shall love the Lord your God with all your heart, and with all your soul, and with all your mind. This is the greatest and first command-ment. And a second is like it: You shall love your neighbor as yourself."* (Matthew 22:37-39)

In a world where we are taught that we are free to live as we choose, that no one has the right to tell us what to do, and that we are to be our own boss it is challenging to be obedient to God's will for us. Jesus encountered similar challenges, but he made the choice to walk in obedience to Our Father's will, and said, *"I do not seek my own will but the will of the one who sent me."* (John 5:30)

Reflection:

So what is it that you place before your obedience to God's will: your spouse?   your children?   relatives?

friends? your job? earning money? the acquisition of material goods? your hobbies?

Do you dedicate a few minutes of your day to God, quietly listening in order to discover His will for you? Maybe you have taken on so much that you do not have time to think about God or His will for you. The end of the day comes along and you are tired and drained of energy so it is hard to dedicate time to God in order to discover His will for your life.

Do you truly love yourself? Are you critical of yourself or judgmental? Do you focus on your imperfections and faults? Do you see the beauty that God has created within you? Do you love others the way you love yourself?

Visualization:

Picture yourself sitting at Jesus' feet. He says to you, *"Do not fear, for I am with you, do not be afraid, for I am your God; I will strengthen you, I will help you."* (Isaiah 41:10) Open your heart to Him, tell Him of all the areas in your life that you have not dedicated to Him, all the ways you have not placed His Father's will before your own, all the ways in which you have not loved yourself or others as He would have you love. Ask Him to help you find the time to come to Him for a few minutes a day to pray and quietly embrace the love He has for you. *"Commit your way to the Lord; trust in him, and he will act."* (Psalm 37:5)

Jesus looks you in the eye and says, *"But with everlasting love I will have compassion on you."* (Isaiah 54:8) He extends His hands and places them on your head. Feel His love and mercy flowing into you. Feel yourself being strengthened and filled with the grace of obedience to God's will. Feel your heart and mind being changed. See yourself as God sees you, beautiful, gifted and loving. Dedicate your body, mind, heart and soul to Him. Ask Jesus to take away your habit of criticizing yourself or others, your tendency to judge and replace those with genuine love and acceptance of yourself and others. Hear the Lord say to you, *"Your sins are forgiven. Your faith has saved you; go in peace."* (Luke 7:48,50)

As you leave Him, see His joy and feel His love for you. *"Great is the Lord and highly to be praised; awesome is he."* (Psalm 96:4 NAB)

Pray:

- ❖ **10 Hail Marys**
- ❖ **Glory Be**
- ❖ **Decade Prayer**
- ❖ **Hail Holy Queen**
- ❖ **O God**
- ❖ **Pardon Prayer**

The Luminous Mysteries

As you pray the Luminous Mysteries allow yourself to be enlightened about who Jesus is through these mysteries of His ministerial life. Jesus said, *"I am the light of the world. Whoever follows me will never walk in darkness but will have the light of life."* (John 8:12) He also said, *"I have come as light into the world, so that everyone who believes in me should not remain in the darkness."* (John 12:46) He came to bring us out of the darkness of sin and death into the light of grace and eternal life. He loved us so much that He sent the Holy Spirit to illuminate our hearts and minds and lead our souls in truth to Him and to Our Father in heaven. Jesus does not intend for our walk with Him to be fraught with difficulty. He said, *"Take my yoke upon you, and learn from me; for I am gentle and humble in heart, and you will find rest for your souls."* (Matthew 11:29) He doesn't burden us with pain and suffering but offers us rest and repose in the midst of our pain and suffering. He offers Himself wholly to us. Perhaps as we walk through these Luminous Mysteries we can in turn offer ourselves body, mind, heart, and soul to Him.

Prayer

Dearest Father, thank You for the gift of Your Son, Jesus Christ. Teach me through His example how to be a child of light and love. Help me to grow in my love for You, for Him and for Your Holy Spirit. Help me to constantly seek You in Your Triune form and help me be open to the gifts of Your Holy Spirit being manifest in my life.

Jesus, help me to be strong and courageous as I allow my heart, mind and soul to be converted. May every day be one in which I seek to know You more fully. Help me to accept Your healing love, forgiveness and compassion. Fortify my love for You in Holy Eucharist.

Heavenly Mother, teach me the way of humble obedience. Help me to trust fully in God's love for me. Help me to love Him more fully each day. Intercede for me that I may have a truly forgiving heart for myself and others. Thank you, dearest Mother for your love and constant intercession.

May the Holy Trinity be praised, honored and glorified always. Amen.

Pray:

- ❖ **Sign of the Cross**
- ❖ **Apostles' Creed**
- ❖ **Hail Mary** (for an increase in faith)
- ❖ **Hail Mary** (for an increase in hope)
- ❖ **Hail Mary** (for an increase in love)
- ❖ **Glory Be**

The First Luminous Mystery
The Baptism in the Jordan

I am baptizing you with water, for repentance, but the one who is coming after me is mightier than I. I am not worthy to carry his sandals. He will baptize you with the holy Spirit and fire.
Then Jesus came from Galilee to John at the Jordan to be baptized by him. John tried to prevent him, saying, "I need to be baptized by you, and yet you are coming to me?" Jesus said to him in reply, "Allow it now, for thus it is fitting for us to fulfill all righteousness." Then he allowed him. After Jesus was baptized, he came up from the water and behold, the heavens were opened for him, and he saw the Spirit of God descending like a dove and coming upon him. And a voice came from the heavens, saying, "This is my beloved Son, with whom I am well pleased." (Matthew 3:11, 13-17 NAB)

Pray:

❖ **Our Father**

There is no virtue traditionally associated with this mystery, but might I suggest a desire to live one's Baptismal promises?

What are our Baptismal promises? They are promises we have publicly made that clarify for us and for others what we believe. We took responsibility for them in our Confirmation and we renew them every Easter season. Here are the questions we are asked to which we verbally respond, "I do."

Do you reject Satan?
And all his works?
And all his empty promises?
Do you believe in God, the Father Almighty, creator of heaven and earth?
Do you believe in Jesus Christ, his only Son, our Lord, who was born of the Virgin Mary was crucified, died, and was buried, rose from the dead, and is now seated at the right hand of the Father?
Do you believe in the Holy Spirit, the holy Catholic church, the communion of saints, the forgiveness of sins, the resurrection of the body, and life everlasting?

Then the priest or deacon says:

God, the all-powerful Father of our Lord Jesus Christ has given us a new birth by water and the Holy Spirit, and forgiven all our sins. May he also keep us faithful to our Lord Jesus Christ for ever and ever.

And we answer, "Amen".

Reflection:

It is easier to believe in God the Father, Jesus His Son, the Holy Spirit, the church, the communion of saints, the forgiveness of sins, resurrection of the body, and life everlasting than it is to reject Satan, all his works and all his empty promises.   This is because Satan is the deceiver, the liar, and a fraud. He tricks us into taking our eyes off God and placing them on ourselves, on the material world, on our relationships. He lures us into a false sense of security in our own abilities and plans and fills our minds with doubts. ***"Discipline yourselves; keep*** *alert. Like a roaring lion your adversary the devil prowls around, looking for someone to devour. Resist him, steadfast in your faith, for you know that your brothers and sisters throughout the world are undergoing the same kinds of suffering."* (1 Peter 5:8)

Satan has some people so deceived that they do not believe he exists. He is a master at perverting the truth. He is constantly reminding us of the misfortunes, troubles, sufferings and frustrations of life, always hoping we'll fall into despair. So, *"Put on the whole armour of God, so that you may be able to stand against the wiles of the devil."* (Ephesians 6:11)

To reject Satan is hard work. It takes a daily commitment to keep our eyes on God, His will for us, and our ultimate goal, everlasting life in union with Him in heaven. We can be sure that God is protecting us from Satan's onslaughts. *"But the one who was born of God protects them, and the evil one does not touch them."* (1 John 5:18)

Remember, if Satan tempted Jesus he'll surely tempt us. Satan knows our weaknesses and vulnerabilities and will do everything in his power to prey upon those. But Jesus has won the victory over Satan, over sin, over death. Of that we can be sure. *"Submit yourselves therefore to God. Resist the devil, and he will flee from you. Draw near to God, and he will draw near to you."* (James 4:7-8)

Visualization:

Picture yourself standing at the edge of the River Jordan. John has just baptized Jesus and you are amazed at what you have just seen and heard. You are the next person waiting to be baptized. As you walk into the water where John and Jesus are standing, you say to

65

Jesus, *"Deal kindly with me for your name's sake; in your generous kindness rescue me; for I am wretched and poor, and my heart is pierced within me."* (Psalm 109:21-22 NAB) Jesus says to you, *"As the Father has loved me, so I have loved you; abide in my love. If you keep my commandments, you will abide in my love."* (John 15:9-10) John dips you backwards into the water and as you come up Jesus says, *"I am the way, and the truth, and the life."* (John 14:6) "Know me, *'And you will know the truth, and the truth will make you free.'"* (John 8:32)

The Holy Spirit within you leads you to tell Jesus of the areas in your life where Satan has been tempting you to take your eyes off God and put them on yourself and the things of the world, the areas in which you have been deceived. With complete conviction you say, *"Get behind me, Satan! You are a stumbling-block to me."* (Matthew 16:23) Jesus reaches out and touches you, saying, "Allow me to fill you with renewed faith and discipline, *'So that Satan may not tempt you through your lack of self-control.'"* (1 Corinthians 7:5) Humbled, you say, *"I give thanks to you, O Lord, with my whole heart."* (Psalm 138:1) *"For the Lord our God the Almighty reigns. Let us rejoice and exult and give him the glory."* (Revelation 19:6-7)

Pray:

- ❖ **10 Hail Marys**
- ❖ **Glory Be**
- ❖ **Decade Prayer**

The Second Luminous Mystery
The Wedding at Cana

On the third day there was a wedding in Cana in Galilee, and the mother of Jesus was there. Jesus and his disciples were also invited to the wedding. When the wine ran short, the mother of Jesus said to him, "They have no wine." And Jesus said to her, "Woman, how does your concern affect me? My hour has not yet come." His mother said to the servers, "Do whatever he tells you." Now there were six stone water jars there for Jewish ceremonial washings, each holding twenty to thirty gallons. Jesus told them, "Fill the jars with water." So they filled them to the brim. Then he told them, "Draw some out now and take it to the headwaiter." So they took it. And when the headwaiter tasted the water that had become wine, without knowing where it came from (although the servers who had drawn the water knew), the headwaiter called the bridegroom and said to him, "Everyone serves good wine first, and then when people have drunk freely, an inferior one; but you have kept the good wine until now." Jesus did this as the beginning of his signs in Cana in Galilee and so revealed his glory, and his disciples began to believe in him. (John 2:1-11 NAB)

Pray:

❖ Our Father

There is no virtue traditionally associated with this mystery, but might I suggest trust in God?

The Psalmist wrote, *"I trust in the Lord, my soul trusts in his word."* (Psalm 130:5) Trusting the Lord is having complete confidence in Him, in His word, in His promises. It is relying and depending on God's love, mercy and grace to provide for all of our needs. *"Blessed is the man who trusts in the Lord, whose hope is in the Lord."* (Jeremiah 17:7)

Reflection:

Trusting the Lord with all our plans, our hopes, and our dreams can be difficult. We can believe in our minds that He cares for us and desires for us to know Him, love Him and serve Him so we can spend eternity with Him in heaven. But believing with our heart and soul, completely, with utter conviction, that's the hard part. We know that He has promised us eternal life if we love Him above all and love our neighbor as ourselves. *"You shall love the Lord, your God, with all your heart, with all your being, with all your strength, and with all your mind, and your neighbor as yourself...do this and you will live."* (Luke 10:27-28)

Trusting is just not easy. It means letting go of our best laid plans, control over how our life is going to be, and letting God choose what will happen and when, believing that He always has our highest and best interest at heart. *"In God I trust without fear."* (Psalm 56:5)

Sometimes it feels like we are falling, falling, falling and we are afraid no one will be there to catch us. But the truth is, God is there and will catch us. He will not only catch us but also hold us close to His heart and protect us, even from ourselves. *"Cast all your worries upon him because he cares for you,"* (1 Peter 5:7) and,

"Trust in the kindness of God forever and ever." (Psalm 52:10)

Remember, trust is a gift and a grace. It grows with use. So put it to good use for there is no one we can trust in more than God. *"Guard this rich trust with the help of the holy Spirit that dwells within us."* (2 Timothy 1:14)

Visualization:

Imagine yourself standing in your living room and it fills with blinding light. Suddenly before you is Jesus of Mercy. His hands are extended towards you and He says, *"Steadfast love surrounds those who trust in the Lord."* (Psalm 32:10) You want to trust Him with everything, but so many in your life have let you down. You decide to take a leap of faith and say, "Jesus, I trust in You." As you say this you begin to share with Him your hopes, your dreams, your plans.

Jesus listens carefully to all you have to say and says, *"May mercy, peace, and love be yours in abundance."* (Jude 1:2) He blesses you and you feel His peace permeating you, filling you to overflowing. You can feel a new sense of trust as the rays of His mercy and love penetrate your whole being. You look at Him and say, *"You are my God, and I will give thanks to you."* (Psalm 118:28) "Thank you, Jesus, I do trust in You."

"Do not worry about anything, but in everything by prayer and supplication with thanksgiving let your requests be made known to God. And the peace of God, which surpasses all understanding, will guard your hearts and your minds in Christ Jesus." (Philippians 4:6-7)

Pray:

- ❖ **10 Hail Marys**
- ❖ **Glory Be**
- ❖ **Decade Prayer**

The Third Luminous Mystery
The Proclamation of the Kingdom

After John had been arrested, Jesus came to Galilee proclaiming the gospel of God: "This is the time of fulfillment. The kingdom of God is at hand. Repent, and believe in the gospel." (Mark 1:14-15 NAB)

Jesus said to them again, "Peace be with you. As the Father has sent me, so I send you." And when he had said this, he breathed on them and said to them, "Receive the holy Spirit. Whose sins you forgive are forgiven them, and whose sins you retain are retained." (John 20:21-23 NAB)

Pray:

❖ **Our Father**

There is no virtue traditionally associated with this mystery, but might I suggest forgiveness?

Forgiveness is an act of the will, not an emotion. It is a choice made to have mercy on another or on oneself. It is imperative that we forgive in order to receive forgiveness. *"If you forgive others their trespasses, your heavenly Father will also forgive you; but if you do not forgive others, neither will your Father forgive your trespasses."* (Matthew 6:14-15)

Forgiveness does not mean we forget the wrongs that have been done to us, but it does mean we let go of the anger, bitterness, hatred, or resentment we carry towards those who have hurt us. *"Put away from you all bitterness and wrath and anger and wrangling and*

75

slander, together with all malice, and be kind to one another, tender-hearted, forgiving one another, as God in Christ has forgiven you." (Ephesians 4:31-32)

Forgiving doesn't deny the other person's responsibility, minimize or justify the wrongs done, but it can bring peace, hope and healing. Instead of holding grudges you might find you can have compassion on and understanding towards those who have hurt you.

We must treat ourselves and others as God has treated us. Jesus said, "For I have set you an example, that you also should do as I have done to you. Just as I have loved you, you also should love one another." (John 13:15,34)

Reflection:

Perhaps the person you need to forgive most is a family member. Maybe a friend or co-worker has upset or hurt you. Maybe someone has abused you or taken advantage of your kindness. Perhaps someone has hurt you horribly with his or her words. Maybe someone has hurt your child(ren), your spouse or another family member. Perhaps someone you love lost their life needlessly in an accident or tragedy.

There are so many reasons for which we need to forgive others. The list could go on and on. Only you know who you need to forgive and why. And, maybe the person you most need to forgive is yourself. Perhaps you may need to forgive someone many times before you have forgiven them completely because the hurts they have caused may be many. The most important thing is taking those first steps of forgiving.

Remember, when questioned about how many times we must forgive Jesus said, "Not seven times, but, I tell you, seventy-seven times." (Matthew 18:22) Meaning we are to forgive others as many times as we are hurt or harmed by them and forgive ourselves every time we hurt or harm ourselves or others.

Visualization:

Imagine yourself sitting in a meadow of wildflowers chatting with Jesus about your life. You are sharing with Him some of the difficulties you have been having with others. He is listening intently as you talk.

He begins to speak, saying, *"Whose sins you forgive are forgiven them, and whose sins you retain are retained."* (John 20:23) As you think about what He has just said, the Holy Spirit starts to show you who you most need to forgive at this time. People's faces start popping into your head. You feel overwhelmed by the number of people and feelings you have.

You look at the Lord and say, *"Do not be far from me."* (Psalm 22:11) *"O my God, in you I trust."* (Psalm 25:2) One by one give the people you see in your mind's eye to the Lord and forgive each one as best you can. As you are working through forgiving, Jesus takes your hand in His and begins pouring His love and mercy into you. You can feel waves of love and compassion washing over you, blessing you. With gentleness of heart He wipes away your fear, your anger, and your pain. He says as you finish, *"I am He who blots out your transgressions for my own sake, and I will not remember your sins."* (Isaiah 43:25)

You thank Him as He hugs you and holds you close to His Sacred Heart. Grace fills you in abundance and you are overcome by how much forgiveness and peace you feel. And you say, *"I will give thanks to you, O Lord, my God, with my whole heart, and I will glorify your name for ever."* (Psalm 108:5)

77

Pray:

- ❖ **10 Hail Marys**
- ❖ **Glory Be**
- ❖ **Decade Prayer**

The Fourth Luminous Mystery
The Transfiguration

After six days Jesus took Peter, James, and John his brother, and led them up a high mountain by themselves. And he was transfigured before them; his face shone like the sun and his clothes became white as light. And behold, Moses and Elijah appeared to them, conversing with him. Then Peter said to Jesus in reply, "Lord, it is good that we are here. If you wish, I will make three tents here, one for you, one for Moses, and one for Elijah." While he was still speaking, behold, a bright cloud cast a shadow over them, then from the cloud came a voice that said, "This is my beloved Son, with whom I am well pleased; listen to him." When the disciples heard this, they fell prostrate and were very much afraid. But Jesus came and touched them, saying, "Rise, and do not be afraid." And when the disciples raised their eyes, they saw no one else but Jesus alone. (Matthew 17:1-8) NAB

Pray:

❖ **Our Father**

There is no virtue traditionally associated with this mystery, but might I suggest conversion?

Conversion in this context is not changing from one faith community to another or finding religion (although it can be a pivotal moment of grace when one is drawn to join the Church) it is changing the mind and heart so that the soul matures, bringing about a noticeable change in behavior, thinking, and/or way of living. This change can be the result of a deeply personal encounter with God, after a moving spiritual experience or the result of deep personal conviction that change is needed. It entails the realization that you are a loved, beautiful, child of God who is cared for. *"So if anyone is in Christ, there is a new creation: everything old has passed away; see, everything has become new!"* (2 Corinthians 5:17)

The new self seeks union with God, continues to transform, is drawn more deeply into prayer, scripture and the sacraments, and chooses to live a holier life. *"You were taught to put away your former way of life, your old self, corrupt and deluded by its lusts, and to be renewed in the spirit of your minds, and to clothe yourselves with the new self, created according to the likeness of God in true righteousness and holiness."* (Ephesians 4:22-24)

Conversion is not just an event it is an ongoing process. It signifies the Holy Spirit at work within us, purifying us, teaching us, and leading us to a deeper relationship with Jesus and God, Our Father. *"May he draw our hearts to himself, that we may walk in his ways and keep his commands, statues, and ordinances."* (1 Kings 8:58)

Reflection:

Many speak of the "born again" experience or "baptism in the spirit" when they have an immediate, deeply moving, personal encounter with God that opens their eyes to a new way of thinking, of living. They feel drawn to the sacraments and to prayer. They feel compelled to change their way of living, to make their choices more aligned with God's commands and the Church's teachings. All this has a profound effect on them and the people they are closest to. Some find their loved ones accepting of the changes but other's find themselves misunderstood, alienated, rejected. Their friends, family and co-workers may call them names and tempt them to return to their former way of living. This can be hurtful and upsetting, but they persevere with courage in a non-judgmental way knowing that the life they are now choosing is a more Christ-like life. *"God did not give us a spirit of cowardice, but rather a spirit of power and love and self-discipline."* (2 Timothy 1:7)

Some do not have the "born again" experience, but they experience a deep conviction that they need to change before or after a sacramental encounter with God. These people too find they have a profound desire to know God more intimately, love Him more deeply, and follow Him more fully. They too can be ostracized, rejected, and led into temptation by those closest to them, the very ones who should be most understanding of their heart's desire. But they choose to be loving, forgiving and understanding because that is what they are called to in Christ Jesus. *"Amen, I say to you, whatever you bind on earth shall be bound in heaven and whatever you loose on earth shall be loosed in heaven."* (Matthew 18:18) They have no desire to cause harm to those around them. They simply want to do the will of God while living in the world. *"Do not love the world or the things in the world. The love of the Father is not in those who love the world; for all that is in the world—the desire of the flesh, the desire of the eyes, the pride in riches—comes not from the Father but from the world. And the world and its desire are passing away, but those who do the will of God live for ever."* (1 John 2:15-17)

Conversion is not an easy process, but it is a fulfilling and wonderful life-long experience that brings a greater sense of peace and joy as you are fortified by the Holy Spirit. So, *"Bear your share of hardships for the gospel with the strength that comes from God."* (2 Timothy 1:8 NAB)

Visualization:

Picture yourself at church. You are sitting in a pew with your eyes closed talking to God in your heart. When you open your eyes you are shocked to see Jesus standing in the pew next to you. You turn to Him and say, *"Create in me a clean heart, O God, and put a new and right spirit within me. Do not cast me away from your presence, and do not take your holy spirit from me. Restore to me the joy of your salvation, and sustain in me a willing spirit."* (Psalm 51:10-12)

Jesus looks at you lovingly and says, *"You are not far from the kingdom of God."* (Mark 12:34) *"If you suffer for doing what is right, you are blessed. Do not fear what they fear, and do not be intimidated."* (1 Peter 3:14)

You share with Jesus the times when those you love and care for have misunderstood you, rejected you for your beliefs or tempted you to live as you used to live before you dedicated yourself to Him. He listens intently and takes your hand in His. You can feel your pain being lifted away and your heart being blessed with strength and courage. You feel a new sense of hope and peace.

Jesus says, *"Anyone whom you forgive, I also forgive."* (2 Corinthians 2:10) One by one, you offer those who have upset you to the Lord for Him to bless and forgive as you also forgive them. God's mercy flows over you in waves and you can feel His compassion filling you. The Holy Spirit renews you and blesses you with new understanding and wisdom. A profound joy fills you and you thank the Lord for His love, compassion and understanding saying, *"I will praise the Lord as long as I live; I will sing praises to my God all my life long."* (Psalm 146:2)

Pray:

- ❖ **10 Hail Marys**
- ❖ **Glory Be**
- ❖ **Decade Prayer**

The Fifth Luminous Mystery
The Institution of the Eucharist

While they were eating, Jesus took bread, said the blessing, broke it, and giving it to his disciples said, "Take and eat; this is my body." Then he took a cup, gave thanks, and gave it to them, saying, "Drink from it, all of you, for this is my blood of the covenant, which will be shed on behalf of many for the forgiveness of sins." (Matthew 26:26-28 NAB)

Pray:

❖ **Our Father**

There is no virtue traditionally associated with this mystery, but might I suggest love for the Eucharist?

At every Mass the priest is united to Christ. It is Jesus who once again offers Himself through the priests hands and voice to His Father, transforming the simple offerings of bread and wine into His body, blood, soul and divinity. As Catholics, who have received our First Communion, we have the opportunity to come forward and receive Jesus just as the apostles received Him at the Last Supper. Then in many churches we are given the blessed opportunity to receive Christ's Precious Blood from the cup of salvation.

In Holy Communion it is not so much that we receive Jesus into ourselves, but that we enter into full union with Him. In consuming Him, He consumes all of us, blessing us, transforming us, healing us. We can receive Jesus in Holy Eucharist every day if disposed to. There are countless Masses said in every city of the world. If we desire to go, we can usually find a Mass time that fits into our busy schedules.

Then there are countless churches that have adoration chapels open 24 hours a day where we can go and sit with Jesus, offering ourselves silently to Him in prayer as He is truly present in Holy Eucharist in the monstrance. These chapels with perpetual adoration are quiet, peaceful places where we can sit with Jesus, loving Him and being loved by Him, blessing Him and being blessed by Him, thanking Him, and listening to Him within our hearts and souls. Adoration is a time of quiet contemplation of simply being with Jesus, adoring Him. It is a time of entering into union with Jesus, a time to offer Jesus all of who we are, all that we need, and all that we hope for and in return receive the grace and strength we need to face the challenges of life.

We can rest assured that if we faithfully receive Jesus in Eucharist we will have eternal life in union with Him, Our heavenly Father, and the Holy Spirit. Jesus has promised it, ***"Whoever eats this bread will live forever."*** (John 6:58) It's up to us to do our part and attend Mass and with a proper disposition to receive Jesus in Holy Eucharist so that He can nourish, forgive, heal, and bring us to everlasting union with Himself.

Reflection:

Maybe you are questioning the teaching of transubstantiation, the changing of bread and wine into the body and blood of Christ. Doubt may have entered your mind and you do not believe fully that the consecrated bread and wine are the true body, blood, soul, and divinity of Jesus. This crisis in faith can be trying. It can cause you to refuse Holy Communion or even leave the Church.

Instead of leaving the Church, ask yourself if you believe what Jesus said is truth or lie? Ask yourself if God, Who is love would deceive you? Seek advice from a parish priest in the confessional or during an office visit. Any priest would be happy to help you through your unbelief. Belief is both a decision and a grace. If in doubt, pray, take action, and remember what Jesus said when questioned about Eucharist, *"Very truly, I tell you, unless you eat the flesh of the Son of Man and drink his blood, you have no life in you. Those who eat my flesh and drink my blood have eternal life, and I will raise them up on the last day; for my flesh is true food and my blood is true drink. Those who eat my flesh and drink my blood abide in me, and I in them. Just as the living Father sent me, and I live because of the Father, so whoever eats me will live because of me."* (John 6:53-57)

Visualizations:

For those who believe:

Picture yourself at Mass. You are kneeling in a pew waiting to go forward to receive Holy Communion. Your eyes are closed and you are preparing your heart to receive Jesus. A brilliant light starts to fill you and your heart beats a little faster. You feel an overwhelming desire for Jesus.

As you come forward in line your mind is focused on how much you love God and how grateful you are to be able to receive the Eucharistic Lord. It is your turn and instead of the priest giving you Communion it is Jesus who gives you His body, blood, soul, and divinity in the consecrated Host. Jesus smiles at you and says, *"This is my body."* (Luke 22:19) As He gives you Eucharist the love you feel is beyond anything you have ever felt.

Mercy and love wash over you in waves.

As you walk back to your pew to kneel down tears of joy begin to fall. Heat fills every part of you. You can feel Jesus' presence consuming you, blessing you, touching you, healing you. You rejoice in amazement for the love God has shown you. In your heart you say, *"O Lord, you are my God: I will exalt you, I will praise your name; for you have done wonderful things."* (Isaiah 25:1)

For those who do not believe:

Picture yourself at mass and the Liturgy of the Eucharist is about to begin. Before you the priest is transformed into Jesus who begins to pray the prayers. As He takes the bread in His hands and raises His eyes to heaven, He says, *"Take and eat; this is my body."* (Matthew 26:26 NAB) Then He continues giving thanks and praise, holding the chalice He says, *"Drink from it, all of you, for this is my blood of the covenant, which will be shed on behalf of many for the forgiveness of sins."* (Matthew 26:27 NAB) As He finishes disbelief flees from you and you are filled with tremendous peace and love. Your heart is moved and your mind is changed.

In your mind's eye, you come forward to receive Holy Communion. Jesus smiles at you. You are overwhelmed with love for Him and by His love for you. As you imagine yourself receiving Holy Communion, heat fills your body and light penetrates every part of your being. You are flooded with God's mercy and tears begin to fall. You realize that you must confess your unbelief so that you can be free to receive Jesus in Holy Eucharist. You make a firm resolve to go to the sacrament of Reconciliation as soon as you can and with a grateful heart you say to Jesus, *"O Lord, you are my God; I will exalt you, I will praise your name; for you have done wonderful things."* (Isaiah 25:1)

Pray:

- ❖ 10 Hail Marys
- ❖ Glory Be
- ❖ Decade Prayer
- ❖ Hail Holy Queen
- ❖ O God
- ❖ Pardon Prayer

The Sorrowful Mysteries

As you pray the Sorrowful Mysteries realize that Jesus' love is a sacrificial love, one of selfless service to others. *"For the Son of Man did not come to be served but to serve and give his life as a ransom for many."* (Mark 10:45) Jesus expected nothing in return for His sacrifice. He simply gave everything for you and me, Jesus said, *"I give you a new commandment: love one another. As I have loved you, so you also should love one another."* (John 13:34) Just as God's love is unconditional so should ours be, one that considers another's needs before our own and is willing to forgive any transgression. Should we love as Christ loves and embrace His healing and forgiveness, we will experience renewed hope, deeper joy, and greater peace in our lives. Remember, as we consider our own suffering and join it to Christ's we can be sure that our suffering is, *"Nothing compared with the glory to be revealed for us."* (Romans 6:18)

Embrace God's healing love for you as you walk through these Sorrowful Mysteries.

Prayer

Dearest Father, I now place myself in Your loving hands. Mold me into the child of light and love that You created me to be. Replace all darkness in my life with the healing light of Your Son, and my Savior, Jesus Christ. Pour forth Your Holy Spirit upon me that I might truly be transformed and fortified.

Dearest Mother Mary, I come before you, seeking your assistance. Place your loving arms around me and carry me to your Son so that He can heal me in those areas of my heart, mind, body, and soul that are in need of His healing touch. Help me, dearest Mother, to resign myself to God's Holy Will. Teach me the value of mortification, which leads to true humility. Intercede for me so that I will have the patience I need to persevere in adversity and the ability to love those who desire to cause me harm. Thank you, dearest Mother for your love and constant intercession.

May the most Holy Trinity be praised, honored, and glorified always! Amen.

Pray:

- ❖ **Sign of the Cross**
- ❖ **Apostles' Creed**
- ❖ **Hail Mary** (for an increase in faith)
- ❖ **Hail Mary** (for an increase in hope)
- ❖ **Hail Mary** (for an increase in love)
- ❖ **Glory Be**

The First Sorrowful Mystery

The Agony in the Garden

Then going out he went, as was his custom, to the Mount of Olives, and the disciples followed him. When he arrived at the place he said to them, "Pray that you may not undergo the test." After withdrawing about a stone's throw from them and kneeling, he prayed, saying, "Father, if you are willing, take this cup away from me; still, not my will but yours be done." And to strengthen him an angel from heaven appeared to him. He was in such agony and he prayed so fervently that his sweat became like drops of blood falling on the ground. (Luke 22:39-44 NAB)

Pray:

❖ **Our Father**

Traditionally associated with this mystery is the virtue of conformity to the will of God.

Conforming our will to God's will is no easy task. It requires surrender, sacrifice, and willingness to take the time to listen to the Holy Spirit speaking quietly within our hearts. As we walk in the Spirit, He guides us in making our moment-to-moment daily decisions as well as the most important decisions of our lives. Jesus said, **"When the Spirit of truth comes, he will guide you into all the truth."** (John 16:13) And He does guide us to truth, that which is the Father will's for us in every aspect of our lives.

We have to realize that there will be times when God will change our plans. In those times we need to remember that Our Father's plans are infinitely wiser and better than any plans we could make for ourselves and that conforming ourselves to His will, will lead us to a deeper, more intimate relationship with Him. If you are willing to trust and obey God and live a holy life, God will reveal Himself to you and direct your steps just as He directed the steps of Jesus. St. Paul wrote, *"**Do not be conformed to this world, but be transformed by the renewing of your minds, so that you may discern what is the will of God—what is good and acceptable and perfect.**"* (Romans 12:2)

There is no better example of conformity to God's will than Jesus. He gave all that He was to Our Father and sacrificed all of Himself so that we could have the opportunity walk in union with Him forever. *"**Although he was a Son, he learned obedience through what he suffered; and having been made perfect, he became the source of eternal salvation for all who obey him.**"* (Hebrews 5:8-9)

Reflection:

What is causing you to ask, "What is Your will for me, O God?" Perhaps there is illness in the family, an elderly parent in need of care, a difficult relationship with a family member or friend. Maybe there has been job loss, financial strain or lack of money. Are you lonely, anxious, stressed or depressed? Is schoolwork or your job overwhelming you? Are you planning a trip, a wedding or an event of some kind?

Sometimes we become overwhelmed by our responsibilities and the problems we face on a daily basis and we are tempted to try to take control of our lives instead of submitting everything to God and then making decisions on how to live. Jesus was overwhelmed but gave us a great example of submission when he said, *"My Father, if it is possible, let this cup pass from me; yet not as I will, but as you will."* (Matthew 26:39 NAB) Are you willing as Jesus was willing to surrender all that you have, all that you are, and all that you plan to do in order that Our Father's will be done in your life?

Visualization:

Imagine yourself sitting at your kitchen table with God the Father. He is lovingly looking at you as He says, *"When you look for me you will find me. Yes, when you seek me with all your heart, you will find me with you."* (Jeremiah 29:12-13 NAB) *"It is My desire that you trust in My will for you. Is there anything you would like to surrender to Me?"*

Take a moment and think of what you would like to entrust to Him. Then, one by one, surrender each thing you would like to give to Him. As you speak, feel the warmth of God's love permeating your heart, mind and soul. Allow His Spirit to illuminate every aspect of your life, filling you with peace.

As He listens to you like the loving Father He is, Jesus comes to join you. He says, *"In the world you will have trouble, but take courage, I have conquered the world."* (John 16:33 NAB) *"Do not love the world or the things of the world. The world and its enticement are passing away. But whoever does the will of God remains forever."* (1 John 2:15,17 NAB) As He finishes speaking He places His hand over your heart. Feel His loving mercy flow over you in waves, blessing you. *"Give thanks to the Lord for he is good."* (Psalm 136:1)

Pray:

- ❖ **10 Hail Marys**
- ❖ **Glory Be**
- ❖ **Decade Prayer**

The Second Sorrowful Mystery

The Scourging

When Pilate saw that he was not succeeding at all, but that a riot was breaking out instead, he took water and washed his hands in the sight of the crowd, saying, "I am innocent of this man's blood. Look to it yourselves." And the whole people said in reply, "His blood be upon us and upon our children." Then he released Barabbas to them, but after he had Jesus scourged, he handed him over to be crucified. (Matthew 27:24-26 NAB)

Pray:

❖ **Our Father**

Traditionally associated with this mystery is the virtue of mortification.

To mortify means to subdue (the body or its needs and desires) by self-denial or discipline. In the extreme it is to self-inflict pain or harm in order to bring the body and soul into subjection to God's will. This kind of mortification was practiced by many of the saints. Very few are called to the extreme, but everyone is called to self-denial and self-discipline. Jesus said, *"If any want to become my followers, let them deny themselves and take up their cross daily and follow me."* (Luke 9:23)

Mortification is a means of curbing bad habits and implanting new life-giving habits, of curbing vices and implanting virtue and grace. It is a dying to self so that the soul can grow in grace and one can become more Christ-like. *"And those who belong to Christ Jesus have crucified the flesh with its passions and desires."* (Galatians 5:24) They have mortified themselves. They have denied their flesh satisfaction out of love for God.

A simple example of mortification is when driving you may be tempted to judge other drivers or name call, offer those moments to God and deny yourself the satisfaction of judging or name-calling. In sacrificing those moments, and giving them to God, your ride is smoother and calmer and you arrive at your destination feeling more loving instead of guilty or ashamed. Another example is not buying that chocolate bar you want while in line at the grocery store. It's a small act, but it is one of self-denial and self-discipline. Remember, when you mortify yourself you should be growing in the fruit of the Spirit *"Love, joy, peace, patience, kindness, generosity, faithfulness, gentleness and self-control."* (Galatians 5: 22-23)

Reflection:

There are so many moments in our lives that we could offer to God, little moments of self-denial or self-discipline that no one but God knows about. For instance when we have moments of rage, jealousy, hatred, judgment, vanity, bragging, selfishness, irritability, lust or greed we could offer those moments to God and not allow ourselves the satisfaction of following through on those behaviors. Or what about when we are tempted to gossip, overeat, drink too much, self-indulge, be impatient? What about choosing to smile when faced with adversity, or being kind to someone who is annoying, or choosing to be in a good mood when you would like nothing more than to brood? We could quietly offer those moments to God and deny ourselves. In any given day there are innumerable opportunities to offer to God for the mortification of our bodies and souls.

Visualization:

Picture Jesus standing before you, wounded and bleeding. His anguish shows in His eyes. He says, *"If the world hates you, be aware that it hated me before it hated you. If you belonged to the world, the world would love you as its own. Because you do not belong to the world, but I have chosen you out of the world— therefore the world hates you. Remember the word that I said to you, 'Servants are not greater than their master.' If they persecuted me, they will persecute you."* (John 15:18-20)

Jesus reaches out and touches you with His bloodstained hand and pours into you the courage and strength you need to be willing to deny yourself and take up your cross daily and follow Him. He says, *"I will never forsake you or abandon you."* (Hebrews 13:5) *"My grace is sufficient for you, for my power is made perfect in weakness."* (2 Corinthians 12:9 NAB)

Take a moment and offer to the Lord the areas of weakness you struggle with on a daily basis. Ask Him to forgive you for the times you have thought He had abandoned you. Allow His mercy to penetrate your heart and mind and His Spirit to fill you with a deep desire to change your behavior. Feel His healing love and forgiveness flow into you, filling you. *"Seek the Lord and his strength; seek his presence continually."* (Psalm 105:4)

Pray:

- ❖ **10 Hail Marys**
- ❖ **Glory Be**
- ❖ **Decade Prayer**

The Third Sorrowful Mystery

The Crowning with Thorns

Then the soldiers of the governor took Jesus inside the praetorium and gathered the whole cohort around him. They stripped off his clothes and threw a scarlet military cloak about him. Weaving a crown out of thorns, they placed it on his head, and a reed in his right hand. And kneeling before him, they mocked him, saying, "Hail, King of the Jews!" They spat upon him and took the reed and kept striking him on the head. And when they had mocked him, they stripped him of the cloak, dressed him in his own clothes, and led him off to crucify him. (Matthew 27:27-31 NAB)

Pray:

❖ **Our Father**

Traditionally associated with this mystery is moral courage or fortitude.

Fortitude is what gives us the strength to do what is right, not because God sees all that we do, but because it is right and will please Him. It is doing right even when facing embarrassment, discrimination, difficulty, danger, disapproval, ridicule, punishment, rejection, or any kind of backlash. It requires listening to that still small voice within that is the Holy Spirit inspiring us to do what is right according to God's law. One who acts with moral courage never expects to receive anything. He or she simply does because doing is right.

God says, *"I hereby command you: be strong and courageous; do not be frightened or dismayed, for the Lord your God is with you wherever you go."* (Joshua 1:9) He promises to be with us no matter what we face on a daily basis. He is always there, guiding us with His Spirit to truth.

Even Jesus faced moments when He stood up for what was right. Remember the story of the woman who committed adultery? The Pharisees wanted to stone her and asked Jesus what he thought. They wanted to trip Him up and have a reason to be able to charge Him with disobeying the law. Instead of agreeing with them he wrote in the dirt and said, *"Let anyone among you who is without sin be the first to throw a stone at her."* (John 8:7) In response to His courage the Pharisees and the crowd walked away. Jesus has been led by the Holy Spirit to challenge them and stand firm in His teaching that no one should judge or condemn another. In fact that scene ends with Jesus saying to the woman, *"Neither do I condemn you. Go your way, and from now on do not sin again."* (John 8:11)

Reflection:

There are so many times when fortitude is needed. When we are called to witness our belief in God, will we? Jesus said, *"Everyone therefore who acknowledges me before others, I also will acknowledge before my Father in heaven; but whoever denies me before others, I also will deny before my Father in heaven."* (Matthew 10:32-33) When we are called to stand up for someone who is being hurt, wronged, or bullied, will we? Jesus said, *"Do to others as you would have them do to you."* (Luke 6:31) When being mocked, ridiculed or punished because we have chosen not to do something that goes against God's laws, will we stand firm? Jesus said, *"Blessed are you when people revile you and persecute you and utter all kinds of evil against you falsely on my account. Rejoice and be glad, for your reward is great in heaven."* (Matthew 5:11-12)

It takes moral courage to face the world we live in and do what is right and good according to God. Remember, *"God is able to make every grace abundant for you, so that in all things, always having all that you need, you may have an abundance for every good work."* (2 Corinthians 9:8 NAB)

Visualization:

Picture yourself there as Jesus is mocked and crowned with thorns. Blood is streaming down His face and His body is wracked with pain. He looks into your eyes and quietly says, *"What do you want me to do for you?"* (Mark 10:51)

Without hesitating, ask Him for the strength to do the Father's will and the grace to stand firm when faced with embarrassment, discrimination, difficulty, danger, disapproval, ridicule, punishment, rejection, or any kind of backlash because you have chosen to do what is right and good. Ask Him for the ability to trust that He will be with you in every situation you face, strengthening you and filling you with His love and understanding.

Jesus says, *"I am with you always."* (Matthew 28:20) *"Receive the Holy Spirit."* (John 20:22) Feel His Spirit flowing into you, fortifying you. Finally, exhausted, He tenderly touches your heart and says to you, *"Keep alert, stand firm in your faith, be courageous, be strong. Let all that you do be done in love."* (1 Corinthians 16:13-14) And they lead Him away.

Pray:

- ❖ **10 Hail Marys**
- ❖ **Glory Be**
- ❖ **Decade Prayer**

The Fourth Sorrowful Mystery
The Carrying of the Cross

As they led him away they took hold of a certain Simon, a Cyrenian, who was coming in from the country; and after laying the cross on him, they made him carry it behind Jesus. A large crowd of people followed Jesus, including many women who mourned and lamented him. Jesus turned to them and said, "Daughters of Jerusalem, do not weep for me; weep instead for yourselves and for your children." (Luke 23:26-28 NAB)

Pray:

❖ **Our Father**

Traditionally associated with this mystery is the virtue of patience in adversity.

Patience is having quiet, steady perseverance in the face of adversity or trial. It is remaining calm, composed, and self-controlled in trying circumstances. It is bearing pain, misfortune or delays with courage and strength. *"For you need endurance, so that when you have done the will of God, you may receive what was promised."* (Hebrews 10:36)

When undergoing temptation, trials, and difficulties we sometimes wonder if God is with us, if He is there to help us. We can lose sight of the reality that He cares for us, is ever-present, and desires for us to be whole, peace-filled, loving children. *"God is our refuge and our strength, an ever-present help in distress."* (Psalm 46:1 NAB) When faced with our daily struggles it is hard to be patient. It is easy to become frustrated and impatient when things are not turning out our way, in our time. But, *"We know that all things work together for good for those who love God, who are called according to his purpose."* (Romans 8:28)

Minor irritations, little annoyances, and setbacks are all a part of life. *"Many are the afflictions of the righteous, but the Lord rescues them from them all."* (Psalm 34:19) In light of eternity these irritations, annoyances and setbacks are insignificant. Remember, *"After you have suffered for a little while, the God of all grace, who has called you to his eternal glory in Christ, will himself restore, support, strengthen, and establish you."* (1 Peter 5:10)

God, our Father, will give us the ability to be kind, thoughtful, compassionate, generous, and loving no matter what difficulties we face. For He calls us to be as patient with others as He has been with us, to bear with one another and forgive each other as He has forgiven us. *"As God's chosen ones, holy and beloved, clothe yourselves with compassion, kindness, humility, meekness, and patience. Bear with one another and, if anyone has a complaint against another, forgive each other; just as the Lord has forgiven you, so you also must forgive."* (Colossians 3:12-13)

In adversity it is easy to become angry, frustrated, anxious, bitter, unkind, agitated, intolerant and/or unforgiving. To be patient and accept what is happening in our lives, whether we like it or not, is far more difficult. We lose sight of the opportunity to join our suffering to Jesus' suffering for our sanctification and that of others. It's not that we are to go looking for opportunities to suffer, but when they arise we are called to embrace them lovingly. *"But rejoice in so far as you are sharing Christ's sufferings, so that you may also be glad and shout for joy when his glory is revealed."* (1 Peter 4:13)

Reflection:

There are so many circumstances in our lives in which it is difficult to remain patient: dealing with a sick family member or facing an illness ourselves; harassment at work or school; a loved one who abuses alcohol or drugs; lack of money or medical insurance; strained or estranged relationships; separation or divorce; loss of job or income; death of a loved one or friend. The list can go on and on. And then there are the annoyances of daily life: traffic; lines; solicitation calls; a crying baby in the movies or a restaurant; waiting for an order in the drive-thru; running late; missing keys or cell phone. And that list could go on as well.

The point is not what annoys us or causes us to become impatient, but rather what are we going to do to change how we react and respond to annoying circumstances and daily difficulties? Jesus said, *"In the world you will have trouble, but take courage, I have conquered the world."* (John 16:33 NAB) We can trust that He will give us all the strength and grace we need in every situation. *"Gracious is the Lord, and righteous; our God is merciful."* (Psalm 116:5)

Jesus calls us to embrace difficulty. *"If any want to become my followers, let them deny themselves and take up their cross daily and follow me."* (Luke 9:23) We are to follow Him with love, patience and forgiveness. *"Let the peace of Christ rule in your hearts."* (Colossians 3:15) *"And whatever you do, in word or deed, do everything in the name of the Lord Jesus, giving thanks to God the Father through him."* (Colossians 3:17)

Visualization:

Picture yourself seated at a table with Jesus. You are discussing with Him the difficult situations in your life. He listens carefully to all that you have to say. He tenderly reaches out and takes your hand. His simple touch begins to fill you with renewed courage and His Spirit fills you with renewed strength. He leans toward you and asks, *"What is it you want me to do for you?"* (Mark 10:36)

Tell Jesus what you want Him to do for you. Ask Him for the patience you need to bear your daily crosses. Ask for the ability to persevere lovingly through adversity. Ask for the joy that comes from uniting your suffering with His for Our Father's glory. Seek His assistance. Trust that He will, according to the will of Our Father, do all that you have asked of Him. For, *"We have this confidence in him, that if we ask anything according to his will, he hears us. And if we know that he hears us in regard to whatever we ask, we know that whatever we ask him for is ours."* (1 John 5:14 NAB)

Feel yourself being renewed. Feel the Holy Spirit touching you with peace, acceptance and joy. *"Rejoice in hope, be patient in suffering, persevere in prayer."* (Romans 12:12)

Pray:

- ❖ **10 Hail Marys**
- ❖ **Glory Be**
- ❖ **Decade Prayer**

The Fifth Sorrowful Mystery
The Crucifixion

So they took Jesus, and carrying the cross himself he went out to what is called the Place of the Skull, in Hebrew, Golgotha. There they crucified him, and with him two others, one on either side, with Jesus in the middle. Pilate also had an inscription written and put on the cross. It read, "Jesus the Nazorean, the King of the Jews." Now many of the Jews read this inscription, because the place where Jesus was crucified was near the city; and it was written in Hebrew, Latin, and Greek. So the chief priests of the Jews said to Pilate, "Do not write 'The King of the Jews,' but that he said, 'I am the King of the Jews.'" Pilate answered, "What I have written, I have written."

When the soldiers had crucified Jesus, they took his clothes and divided them into four shares, a share for each soldier. They also took his tunic, but the tunic was seamless, woven in one piece from the top down. So they said to one another, "Let's not tear it, but cast lots for it to see whose it will be," in order that the passage of scripture might be fulfilled that says:

"They divided my garments among them,
and for my vesture they cast lots."

This is what the soldiers did. Standing by the cross of Jesus were his mother and his mother's sister, Mary the wife of Clopas, and Mary of Magdala. When Jesus saw his mother and the disciple there whom he loved, he said to his mother, "Woman, behold, your son." Then he said to the disciple, "Behold, your mother." And from that hour the disciple took her into his home.

After this, aware that everything was now finished, in order that the scripture might be fulfilled, Jesus said, "I thirst." There was a vessel filled with common wine. So they put a sponge soaked in wine on a sprig of hyssop and put it up to his mouth. When Jesus had taken the wine, he said, "It is finished." And bowing his head, he handed over the spirit. (John 19:16-30 NAB)

Pray:

❖ **Our Father**

Traditionally associated with this mystery is the virtue of love of enemies.

Jesus said, *"But I say to you, Love your enemies and pray for those who persecute you, so that you may be children of your Father in heaven; for he makes his sun rise on the evil and on the good, and sends rain on the righteous and on the unrighteous. For if you love those who love you, what reward do you have?"* (Matthew 5:44-46) And, *"Bless those who curse you, pray for those who abuse you."* (Luke 6:28)

It is crucial to understand that love is not a feeling. Love is an act of the will. To love another is to have their welfare and well being at heart. It is to will them goodness and good things always.

Loving our enemies is blessing them with mercy and forgiveness even if they hate us, desire to harm us or wish evil upon us. It is striving to go against our natural inclination to become angry or vengeful, bitter, resentful or spiteful and choosing to be life giving and merciful, loving even when it feels like it is impossible to do so. Love of enemies is not an ideal we strive for, but rather a way of life that we choose because we are commanded to it. Jesus said, *"Love your enemies, do good to those who hate you."* (Luke 6:27)

A large part of loving our enemies is forgiving them and choosing not to harbor hatred or resentment against them. Jesus chose to forgive His enemies when he said, **"Father, forgive them; for they do not know what they are doing."** (Luke 23:34) We can choose to forgive, too. That doesn't mean we will forget what has been done to us, but that we have chosen to love and not bear anger or resentment against another. Remember, **"Whenever you stand praying, forgive, if you have anything against anyone; so that your Father in heaven may also forgive you your trespasses."** (Mark 11:25)

Forgiveness can begin with saying within our hearts and minds, "I choose to forgive ____ for ____." Later, it may become words spoken directly to that person, a phone call, or a letter written to them extending forgiveness. How far you go with forgiving depends on you. There may be circumstances that make it impossible or dangerous for you to physically forgive someone. In those situations write a letter, read it to yourself, offer it to God then burn it. When choosing how far you are willing to go to forgive, remember how far Jesus went to forgive you.

And what if you are your own worst enemy? Are you willing to love yourself and forgive yourself as God loves and forgives you, completely?

Reflection:

Who are your enemies? Are you your own worst enemy?

Perhaps you have been abused emotionally, psychologically, physically or sexually. Maybe you have been raped or robbed of your possessions or reputation. Someone may have spread vicious rumors about you, slandered you, or spread gossip about you or your loved ones. Maybe you have faced prejudice, misunderstanding, bullying, racism or discrimination. Perhaps you have been lied to or misled by someone you trusted. Maybe someone has been condescending, patronizing or arrogant towards you. Someone may have mistreated you at work or fired you from a job. Perhaps someone has committed a crime against you or murdered or killed a friend or loved one.

Visualization:

Picture yourself standing at the foot of the cross. It is dark out and the wind is blowing. Off to the side you see Mary and John. Looking up you see Jesus whose body is torn, broken and bleeding. Jesus looks down on you with tenderness and asks, *"Do you love me?"* (John 21:16) You answer Him, *"Lord, you know everything; you know that I love you."* (John 21:17)

He then says to you, ***"This is my commandment, that you love one another as I have loved you. No one has greater love than this, to lay down one's life for one's friends."*** (John 15:12-13) ***"Do not be overcome by evil, but overcome evil with good."*** (Romans 12:21) ***"Love your enemies and do good to them."*** (Luke 6:35 NAB)

As He finishes speaking He closes His eyes and rests. You can feel His love penetrating your heart and filling it with conviction. Offer Jesus your anger, bitterness, resentment and hatred. Accept the grace to begin forgiving those whom you have considered your enemies. One by one picture them in your mind's eye and tell them you forgive them. Offer them to Jesus for His blessing and forgiveness. Allow the grace of God the Father's love to fill your heart. Forgive yourself and, ***"Give thanks to the Lord, for he is good, for his mercy*** *endures forever."* (Daniel 3:89)

Once more you look at Jesus. He is near death. He looks at you again with tenderness His breathing is pained. Finally, broken, He cries out, *"Father, into your hands I commend my spirit"* (Luke 23:46) and He dies.

Pray:

- ❖ **10 Hail Marys**
- ❖ **Glory Be**
- ❖ **Decade Prayer**
- ❖ **Hail Holy Queen**
- ❖ **O God**
- ❖ **Pardon Prayer**

The Glorious Mysteries

As you pray the Glorious Mysteries keep in mind the ultimate healing, life everlasting in heaven. The healing when our souls are clean and pure and enter into eternal glory with God the Father, the Son and the Holy Spirit, along with Mary, the angels and all those who have entered into heaven before us. Our job here on earth is to know, love and serve God in every way possible so that we can be united with Him forever in heaven. Eternal union with God is our ultimate goal. It is our hope that we will be touched by the everlasting love of God and brought into the glorious peace of heaven. God wants healing and wholeness for us here and in heaven. So, *"Keep yourselves in the love of God; look forward to the mercy of our Lord Jesus Christ that leads to eternal life."* (Jude 1:21) For, *"Whoever believes in the Son has eternal life."* (John 3:36)

Prayer

Dearest Father, I now place myself in Your loving hands. Mold me into the child of light and love You created me to be. Help me to grow in faith, hope and wisdom so that I may die a happy death and enter into full union in heaven with You, Your Son, and the Holy Spirit.

Sweet Jesus, pour forth Your healing love upon me. Replace any darkness in my life with Your light and heal those areas of my heart, mind, body and soul that are in need of Your healing touch. Allow

Your Spirit to flow over me, filling me with peace and joy.

Heavenly Mother, I come before you, seeking your assistance. Carry me to the Father. Present me to Him asking that I become the faith-filled, hopeful, wise child He wants me to be. Thank you, Mother, for your love and constant intercession.

May the most Holy Trinity be praised, honored and glorified always. Amen.

Pray:

- ❖ **Sign of the Cross**
- ❖ **Apostles' Creed**
- ❖ **Hail Mary** (for an increase in faith)
- ❖ **Hail Mary** (for an increase in hope)
- ❖ **Hail Mary** (for an increase in love)
- ❖ **Glory Be**

The First Glorious Mystery

The Resurrection

After the sabbath, as the first day of the week was dawning, Mary Magdalene and the other Mary came to see the tomb. And behold, there was a great earthquake; for an angel of the Lord descended from heaven, approached, rolled back the stone, and sat upon it. His appearance was like lightning and his clothing was white as snow. The guards were shaken with fear of him and became like dead men. Then the angel said to the women in reply, "Do not be afraid! I know that you are seeking Jesus the crucified. He is not here, for he has been raised just as he said. Come and see the place where he lay. Then go quickly and tell his disciples, 'He has been raised from the dead, and he is going before you to Galilee; there you will see him.' Behold, I have told you." Then they went away quickly from the tomb, fearful yet overjoyed, and ran to announce this to his disciples. And behold, Jesus met them on their way and greeted them. They approached, embraced his feet, and did him homage. Then Jesus said to them, "Do not be afraid. Go tell my brothers to go to Galilee, and there they will see me."
(Matthew 28:1-10 NAB)

Pray:

❖ Our Father

Traditionally associated with this mystery is the virtue of faith.

Faith is defined as complete belief, trust or confidence in someone or something for which there is no tangible truth. It is conviction, a confident assurance deep within the heart, mind and soul that propels one forward toward an invisible being or goal. *"Now faith is the assurance of things hoped for, the conviction of things not seen."* (Hebrews 11:1)

Faith is a grace freely given by God to anyone who chooses to embrace it. *"For by grace you have been saved through faith, and this is not your own doing; it is the gift of God— not the result of works, so that no one may boast."* (Ephesians 2:8-9) We can do nothing to earn faith. Faith is freely given and must be freely received. But we can do works that strengthen our faith: our belief that God loves us; our understanding that God wills for us to obey His commandments; our belief in His Son and dedication to following His teachings; and, our acceptance of the gifts of the Holy Spirit. *"And without faith it is impossible to please God, for whoever would approach him must believe that he exists and that he rewards those who seek him."* (Hebrew 11:6)

God wants us to rely upon Him, to trust Him in everything, to confidently believe that He will fulfill His promises to us. He does not want us to worry or be afraid. He has promised to take care of our every need. We need the grace of faith to embrace these truths. *"For in Christ Jesus you are all children of God through faith."* (Galatians 3:26)

Reflection:

At some point in life most people have a crisis of faith. A tragedy happens, difficulties abound, someone from the church community does something upsetting or hurtful and next thing you know you are questioning what you believe and why. Some people go through this more than others, but it happens. And when it does, what will our response be? Will we, *"Trust in the Lord,"* (Psalm 4:6) or will we doubt and think, *"I do believe; help my unbelief!"* (Mark 9:24)

It is difficult to, *"Trust in the Lord with all your heart,"* (Proverbs 3:5) but we are called to, *"Fight the good fight, having faith and a good conscience."* (1 Timothy 1:19) We are called to believe that everything will work towards our greater good according to God's will. Everything can be seen as an opportunity to grow in faith. So, when your faith is tested, *"Trust in the Lord, your God, and you will be found firm."* (2 Chronicles 20:20 NAB) *"For we walk by faith, not by sight."* (2 Corinthians 5:7)

Visualization:

Imagine yourself sitting with Jesus. You are discussing issues that you have with your faith or your faith community. He looks right at you and says, *"Do not fear or lose heart."* (2 Chronicles 20:17 NAB) *"I will not fail you or forsake you. Be strong and courageous."* (Joshua 1:5-6)

Take a moment and quietly offer the Lord all the areas in which you are struggling. Allow Him to take them from you one by one as you say to Him, *"Relieve the troubles of my heart, and bring me out of my distress. Consider my affliction and my trouble, and forgive all my sins."* (Psalm 25:17-18) Feel the Lord's forgiveness flowing out to you. Extend forgiveness to any people in your faith community that have hurt you or upset you in any way.

Say to the Lord, *"Teach me your way, O Lord, that I may walk in your truth; give me an undivided heart."*

(Psalm 86:11) Open your heart and mind to new wisdom and understanding that only He can give through the Holy Spirit. See what you were struggling with through new eyes. Remember, *"The wisdom from above is first pure, then peaceable, gentle, willing to yield, full of mercy and good fruits, without a trace of partiality or hypocrisy."* (James 3:17)

Pray:

- ❖ **10 Hail Marys**
- ❖ **Glory Be**
- ❖ **Decade Prayer**

The Second Glorious Mystery

The Ascension

While they were still speaking about this, he stood in their midst and said to them, "Peace be with you." But they were startled and terrified and thought that they were seeing a ghost. Then he said to them, "Why are you troubled? And why do questions arise in your hearts? Look at my hands and my feet, that it is I myself. Touch me and see, because a ghost does not have flesh and bones as you can see I have." And as he said this, he showed them his hands and his feet. While they were still incredulous for joy and were amazed, he asked them, "Have you anything here to eat?" They gave him a piece of baked fish; he took it and ate it in front of them. He said to them, "These are my words that I spoke to you while I was still with you, that everything written about me in the law of Moses and in the prophets and psalms must be fulfilled." Then he opened their minds to understand the scriptures. And he said to them, "Thus it is written that the Messiah would suffer and rise from the dead on the third day and that repentance, for the forgiveness of sins, would be preached in his name to all the nations, beginning from Jerusalem. You are witnesses of these things. And behold I am sending the promise of my Father upon you; but stay in the city until you are clothed with power from on high."
Then he led them out as far as Bethany, raised his hands, and blessed them. As he blessed them he parted from them and was taken up to heaven. (Luke 24:36-51 NAB)

Pray:

❖ **Our Father**

Traditionally associated with this mystery is the virtue of hope.

Hope is defined as a feeling of expectation and desire for a certain thing to happen. But biblical hope is not just a feeling of expectation. It is a confident conviction that what is hoped for will indeed come to pass. It is trust that what God has promised will be, guaranteed.

Hope sustains us through any crisis of faith, temptation or trial that seems too overwhelming. It is a grace given to us by God through the Holy Spirit that propels us towards God's promise to us and our final goal as Christians, eternal union with Him in heaven. ***"But when the kindness and generous love of God our savior appeared, not because of any righteous deeds we had done but because of his mercy, he saved us through the bath of rebirth and renewal by the holy Spirit, whom he richly poured out on us through Jesus Christ our savior, so that we might be justified by his grace and become heirs in hope of eternal life."*** (Titus 3:4-7 NAB)

Reflection:

Despair is giving up all hope. If we choose to fall into despair we choose to completely give up on God, on all that He has promised in His love and mercy, and on everlasting life in heaven. What a dreadful way to be, hopeless, not believing in God, not believing in a better future, and not believing in eternal life. If we have no hope what are we living for?

When the temptation to give up hope arises, we might ask ourselves, "What am I hoping for? In whom do I hope? What can I do to boost my hope?" Then listen to that still small voice within that is leading you to truth and do what you believe you should do to foster your hope. *"Be strong, and let your heart take courage, all you who wait for the Lord."* (Psalm 31:24)

We can trust that God's love and mercy are greater than our sinfulness and that God will forgive us whenever we ask. *"If we acknowledge our sins, he is faithful and just and will forgive our sins and cleanse us from every wrongdoing."* (1 John 1:9 NAB) There is never a time when it is too hard for the soul to cooperate with grace because it always has a choice. *"And God is able to provide you with every blessing in abundance, so that by always having enough of everything, you may share abundantly in every good work."* (2 Corinthians 9:8) Grace is there and abounds where sin abounds. *"Where sin increased, grace overflowed all the more."* (Romans 5:20 NAB) There is no trial or affliction that cannot help us grow in hope. Bear in mind that, *"Suffering produces endurance, and endurance produces character, and character produces hope, and hope does not disappoint us, because God's love has been poured into our hearts through the Holy Spirit that has been given to us."* (Romans 5:3-5)

Visualization:

Picture the Lord seated on a rock. He is teaching and many have gathered around to listen. He looks directly at you and says, *"You are worried and distracted about many things."* (Luke 10:41) *"Do not give yourself over to sorrow, and do not distress yourself deliberately. A joyful heart is life itself, and rejoicing lengthens one's life span."* (Sirach 30:21-22)

As you think about how you should respond, He rises. He walks over to where you are and gently places His hand over your heart. As He does so, you are filled with the desire to share with Him all that has been draining you of hope. You say to Him, *"For you, O Lord, are my hope, my trust."* (Psalm 71:5) *"My hope is in you."* (Psalm 39:7) Jesus says, *"You are not far from the kingdom of God."* (Mark 12:34) *"Rejoice in hope, be patient in suffering, persevere in prayer."* (Romans 12:12)

You are moved and realize there are many things for which you need the Lord's forgiveness and you say, *"O God, according to your steadfast love; according to your abundant mercy blot out my transgressions. Wash me thoroughly from my iniquity, and cleanse me from my sins."* (Psalm 51:2) Jesus takes you into His arms and pours forth His Spirit upon you, filling you with courage, strength, joy and peace. His love and mercy envelope you and you are filled with renewed hope. He holds you an arms length away from Him, His hands resting gently on your shoulders and says, *"I have loved you with an everlasting love."* (Jeremiah 31:3) *"Peace I leave with you; my peace I give to you."* (John 14:27) And He quietly walks away from you.

"May the God of hope fill you with all joy and peace in believing, so that you may abound in hope by the power of the Holy Spirit." (Romans 15:13)

Pray:

- ❖ **10 Hail Marys**
- ❖ **Glory Be**
- ❖ **Decade Prayer**

The Third Glorious Mystery
The Descent of the Holy Spirit

When the time for Pentecost was fulfilled, they were all in one place together. And suddenly there came from the sky a noise like a strong driving wind, and it filled the entire house in which they were. Then there appeared to them tongues as of fire, which parted and came to rest on each one of them. And they were all filled with the holy Spirit and began to speak in different tongues, as the Spirit enabled them to proclaim. (Acts 2:1-4 NAB)

Pray:

❖ **Our Father**

Traditionally associated with this mystery is openness to the gifts of the Holy Spirit.

What are the gifts of the Holy Spirit? They are wisdom, knowledge, faith, healing, mighty deeds (miracles), prophecy, discernment of spirits, tongues, and interpretation of tongues. These gifts are given by the Holy Spirit in the sacrament of Baptism and fortified through the sacrament of Confirmation. St. Paul wrote, *"To each is given the manifestation of the Spirit for the common good. To one is given through the Spirit the utterance of wisdom, and to another the utterance of knowledge according to the same Spirit, to another faith by the same Spirit, to another gifts of healing by the one Spirit, to another the working of miracles, to another prophecy, to another the discernment of spirits, to another various kinds of tongues, to another interpretation of tongues. All these are activated by one and the same Spirit, who allots each one individually just as the Spirit chooses."* (1 Corinthians 12:7-11) There is a second scripture that speaks of the gifts of the Holy Spirit. *"The spirit of the Lord shall rest on him, the spirit of wisdom and understanding, the spirit of counsel and might, the spirit of knowledge and the fear of the Lord."* (Isaiah 11:2) Traditionally added to these is the gift of piety.

An individual may have one or many of these gifts manifest in their lives at different times as the Spirit leads. The Holy Spirit determines what gifts will become active, within whom, when, and for what purpose. It is our job to be open and willing to embrace each of the gifts of the Holy Spirit so that God's love can flow freely from within us out to others. We need only ask for the ability to be open and willing and the gifts will become manifest as God desires for our edification and the edification of the Church. *"If you then, who are evil, know how to give good gifts to your children, how much more will the heavenly Father give the Holy Spirit to those who ask him!"* (Luke 11:13) We are to, *"Pursue love and strive for the spiritual gifts"* (1 Corinthians 14:1) because, *"Now we have received not the spirit of the world, but the Spirit that is from God, so that we may understand the gifts bestowed on us by God."* (1 Corinthians 2:12)

Reflection:

Perhaps you have encountered someone who in their zeal for the Holy Spirit scared you away from the gifts of the Holy Spirit. Maybe you went to a prayer group or conference and felt out of place or upset because certain gifts confused you or did not manifest for you. Maybe you have judged people who are open to the gifts of the Holy Spirit and you think they are delusional or acting outside the teachings of the Church. Maybe you have been misled and believe the only ones who can minister in the gifts of the Holy Spirit are priests, deacons, and religious brothers and sisters. Perhaps you are afraid, leery or skeptical about the gifts of the Holy Spirit or you're concerned about how others will perceive you if you allow them to be evident in your life? Maybe you have prayed for a certain gift and it has not manifested as you wished. Perhaps you have been jealous or envious of someone else's spiritual gifts. Maybe for some reason you have decided that God does not want to use you to edify others or build up His Church.

Visualization:

Imagine yourself seated at a long table with all the apostles, Mary, and the other women. It is late in the afternoon and you are in the upper room in Jerusalem praying and awaiting the time when Jesus would return to baptize you all in the Holy Spirit. Suddenly from heaven there comes a strong wind and tongues of fire descend, parting and resting on each of you. Your heart is filled to overflowing with peace and love, your mind is opened and filled with wisdom and understanding. You realize that you have been blessed with an outpouring of the Holy Spirit. Your heart feels renewed and you have no fear. Jesus shows Himself to all of you and you feel overwhelming peace. He says, ***"Do not let your hearts be troubled, and do not let them be afraid."*** (John 14:27) He reminds you all of your mission to serve one another and bear fruit. Then He blesses all of you and is then taken into heaven.

"Be glad and rejoice, for the Lord has done great things!" (Joel 2:21)

Pray:

- ❖ **10 Hail Marys**
- ❖ **Glory Be**
- ❖ **Decade Prayer**

The Fourth Glorious Mystery
The Assumption

"A great sign appeared in the sky, a woman clothed with the sun, with the moon under her feet." (Revelation 12:1 NAB)

Pray:

❖ **Our Father**

Traditionally associated with this mystery is the grace of a happy death.

A happy death and eternal life are our final goals for this life. We can trust in these words, *"And this is what he promised us, eternal life."* (1 John 2:25)

A happy death is one that is immersed in the mercy and peace of Christ. It is one filled with grace and light. A happy death would be one in which you are greeted by Jesus, Mary, the angels or the saints and escorted to everlasting life. It may be one in which you are surrounded by those you love, being encouraged to let go of this life and enter into the next. It may be one in which the sacrament of the Anointing of the Sick has been received. It is a joyous occasion and yet an occasion that will bring sorrow. It is a time of thanksgiving for a life well lived, one in which God's love was made manifest. *"Keep yourselves in the love of God; look forward to the mercy of our Lord Jesus Christ that leads to eternal life."* (Jude 1:21)

Jesus has promised eternal life to those who love Him and obey his commandments. *"Very truly, I tell you, anyone who hears my word and believes him who sent me has eternal life, and does not come under judgment, but has passed from death to life."* (John 5:24) And He also said, *"This is indeed the will of my Father, that all who see the Son and believe in him may have eternal life; and I will raise them up on the last day."* (John 6:40)

Reflection:

Why do so many people fear death? If we believe in life after death, then death is merely a transition into another form of reality. That reality most likely is one of eternal love, peace, and happiness. To have an eternal reality of pain and suffering would mean that one has to completely turn away from God, who is love, and choose to be aligned with Satan and all his ways. That is unlikely for most people. So fearing death would seem to be unreasonable or inappropriate.

Some people fear that when they die, they cease to exist. If that were the case, why fear? There is nothingness, no joy, no pain, no existence at all. So, why be afraid?

Other people fear eternal punishment from God for their sins. But, why? If they frequent Reconciliation, attend Mass regularly, receive Eucharist frequently, they really have nothing to fear because God has forgiven their mortal sins, their venial sins and they move from being out of a state of grace back into a state of grace.

Suppose you were to die right now. You arrive in Purgatory. What a blessing because instead of wondering whether Heaven really exists, you know with certainty it does indeed exist and you know without any doubt, one day you will find yourself in Heaven, purified and full of love and peace and joy. You won't be stuck in Purgatory forever. Countless souls offer their prayers and suffering for the souls in most need of God's mercy and for the souls in Purgatory. So if you have tried to live your earthly life as a good Catholic Christian one day you will be moved from Purgatory into Heaven.

"God is love, and those who abide in love abide in God, and God abides in them." (1 John 4:16) God the Father sent His Son, our Lord into the world to save sinners, not condemn them to everlasting death. *"God's love was revealed among us in this way: God sent his only Son into the world so that we might live through him. In this is love, not that we loved God but that he loved us and sent his Son to be the atoning sacrifice for our sins."* (1 John 4:9-10)

To believe that God would condemn a loving person contradicts Who He is, the perfect being Who is love. Yes, there is a hell for those who freely choose it. But that is not the norm. Certainly there are people who choose this, but your average Catholic Christian is not one who will. Your average Catholic Christian tries where they are in life, with the knowledge and understanding they have, to love God and love others as best they can. They are not hateful and vindictive, choosing a life devoid of love.

The choice of how you view death is yours. Choose wisely, based on the promises God has made and be at peace. Live today as if it were your last day on earth, loving as best you can, yourself and those around you because, *"The gift of God is eternal life in Christ Jesus our Lord."* (Romans 6:23)

Visualization:

Imagine yourself at the moment of death. You are surrounded by those you love most. They are telling you how much they love you and that they want you to be at peace. You love them and don't want to let go, but

151

suddenly, God the Father, Jesus, Mary and those you love who have died before you are standing around you encouraging you to let go of your earthly body. As they do, you take Jesus' hand and all fear of the unknown leaves you. You are filled with joy and peace. Your loved ones all come to you and hug you, so happy to be reunited with you. God the Father smiles at you and Mary takes your other hand.

You find yourself in the most beautiful place you have ever seen. The colors are so vivid and crisp. You enter God's throne room and you find yourself kneeling before the Father. He asks you only one question, "How have you allowed Me to love you and love Myself in others through you?" Your life begins to play before you. People you touched knowingly and unknowingly come forward to bless you. You are aware of every moment you have allowed God to love through you. A peace you have never known fills you to overflowing and complete joy envelops you.

God smiles at you and welcomes you with open arms into His heavenly kingdom. In your joy, you reconnect with all your loved ones and praise and glorify God singing, ***"Blessing and glory and wisdom and thanksgiving and honour and power and might be to our God for ever and ever!"*** (Revelation 7:12)

Pray:

- ❖ **10 Hail Marys**
- ❖ **Glory Be**
- ❖ **Decade Prayer**

The Fifth Glorious Mystery
The Coronation

"And on her head a crown of twelve stars." (Revelation 12:1 NAB)

Pray:

❖ **Our Father**

Traditionally associated with this mystery is union with Mary.

But what does union with Mary, our Mother mean? It simply means placing ourselves in the loving arms of our Mother who loves us and wants all good things for us in Christ Jesus and allowing her to embrace us fully as her children. It is trusting in Mary to carry us tenderly to the throne of Our Father and place us lovingly there in order for His will to be made manifest in our lives. It is allowing her to teach us how to magnify God in the ordinariness of our daily lives. It is uniting our "Yes" to her "Yes" and together walking in the light and grace of the Holy Spirit through the life God wills for us so that we can enter into full union with Him and with her for eternity.

Reflection:

Unfortunately some people may find it hard to seek union with Mary because they have not had a strong, loving relationship with their own mother. Some people may have a tough time trusting that Mary cares for them because they were not cared for and cherished, as they should have been by their mother. If abused or neglected by their mother, they may have a very hard time believing there is a mother who desires to gently guide them, teach them, and tenderly love them.

Our mothers should be the first person we learn to trust. They are the ones who should love us more than anyone on earth. They should be our fiercest protectors, our biggest encouragers, and our most avid fans. They should be the ones who teach us to be loving and gentle towards others, the ones who teach us empathy and kindness. Our mothers should be our staunchest advocates. They should be the ones who teach us respect by the way they treat themselves and others. Our mothers should always want what is best for us in every situation. They should be the ones who teach us selflessness and humility by the way they give of themselves to others and by their strength and courage in the face of life's struggles and difficulties. Our mothers should be our greatest disciplinarians and best role models. Simply put, our mother's should love us as God has loved them.

Visualization:

Picture yourself standing in your family home when you were young with Jesus. Ask Him to walk with you into the most painful memories you have with your mother. As you enter into these memories with the Lord, He puts His arm around you and engulfs you with His love and His peace. He hugs you and holds you close to His Sacred Heart. He walks with you through your memories one by one and wipes away your tears, calms your fears, removes your pain and hurt, and fills you with His love and acceptance. As He does this He extends His forgiveness to your mother and says to you, ***"When you stand to pray, forgive anyone against whom you have*** *a grievance, so that your heavenly Father may in turn forgive you your transgressions."* (Mark 11:25) Realizing you must forgive your mother, you quietly say, "I forgive her." Light begins to penetrate your heart and mind and you can feel God the Father's love filling you.

Suddenly, Mary is standing with you. She smiles and opens her arms to you offering you her love and protection. You run into the safety of her arms. Let her tenderness touch your heart and feel her love soothing your hurt and pain. Let her fill you with the mother's love you have needed. Thank her for her gentle and abiding love. She gently hands you to her Son. As Jesus takes you in His arms, He fills you to overflowing with a deep and genuine forgiveness for your mother, a new understanding of her when she hurt you. Thank Him for opening your eyes to see her inability to give you what you needed most, her love, understanding, and protection. Thank Him for helping you have mercy on your mother.

"In all circumstances give thanks, for this is the will of God for you in Christ Jesus." (2 Thessalonians 5:18)

Pray:

- ❖ **10 Hail Marys**
- ❖ **Glory Be**
- ❖ **Decade Prayer**
- ❖ **Hail Holy Queen**
- ❖ **O God**
- ❖ **Pardon Prayer**

Concluding Prayer

Thank You, Heavenly Father, for the blessings you have bestowed upon me. Thank You for Your love and tender care as I prayed this Rosary.

Thank You, Jesus, for Your infinite mercy and forgiveness. Continue to heal me and bless my life.

Thank You, Holy Spirit, for bestowing Your graces upon me and filling me with peace.

Thank you, Sweet Mother, for holding me close and interceding for me before the Blessed Trinity.

May the Holy Trinity always be honored and glorified in my life. Amen.

Notes

Quotes about the Rosary from Saints

1. http://stmary.sg
2. http://whitelilyoftrinity.com
3. http://whitelilyoftrinity.com
4. http://whitelilyoftrinity.com
5. http://www.scripturalrosary.org
6. http://stmary.sg
7. http://stmary.sg
8. http://stmary.sg
9. http://whitelilyoftrinity.com
10. http://www.catholicbible101.com
11. http://www.tfpstudentaction.org
12. http://www.tfpstudentaction.org

Quotes about the Rosary from Popes

1. http://whitelilyoftrinity.com
2. http://whitelilyoftrinity.com
3. http://www.catholicbible101.com
4. http://www.catholicbible101.com
5. http://www.catholicbible101.com
6. ROSARIUM VIRGINIS MARIAE
7. http://www.scripturalrosary.org
8. http://www.scripturalrosary.org
9. ROSARIUM VIRGINIS MARIAE
10. MARIALIS CULTUS
11. MAGNAE DEI MATRIS
12. INGRAVESCENTIBUS MALIS
13. LAETITIAE SANCTAE
14. CHRISTI MATRI
15. AD CAELI REGINAM

ABOUT THE AUTHOR

Ann Fitch is a Roman Catholic mother and wife who is seeking a more intimate relationship with God, growing in her faith, and learning more each day about what it means to be a Catholic Christian.

Ann lives in Arizona with her husband and two daughters. Please visit Ann's web site and her blog:

www.annfitch.com

www.catholic-christian.tumblr.com

35256425R00100

Printed in Great Britain
by Amazon